LIBROTANGO

VOLUME I

By the same author

POETRY

Melody's Fool
Improvisations
Rhapsodies

TRANSLATION

Giacomo Leopardi:
Cantos

AS EDITOR

James Thomson (B. V.):
Complete Poems

AS DESIGNER

S. W. Erdnase:
The Expert at the Card Table
First Edition Facsimile

Librotango

· VOLUME 1 ·

TRANSLATED BY
JAKE SPATZ

CHARLES & WONDER
MMXXII

CHARLES & WONDER
PURVEYORS OF FINE LITERATURE
ARLINGTON, VA

Librotango
Volume 1

Book and cover design by Jake Spatz

First hardcover edition
ISBN 978-1-937620-23-3

Published simultaneously
in paperback

CONTENTS

Foreword 9
Introduction 11
Milonguita 18
Mano a mano 20
Caminito 24
Alma en pena 26
Madreselva 30
Cambalache 34
No me pregunten por qué 38
El día que me quieras 42
Alma del bandoneón 46
Nostalgias 50
Quiero verte una vez más 54
Tinta roja 58
Qué te importa que te llore 62
Malena 66
Pedacito de cielo 70
Gricel 74
Mañana zarpa un barco 76
Así se baila el tango 80
Los mareados 84
Percal 86
Esta noche de luna 90
Nada 94
Llueve otra vez 96
Garras 98
Rondando tu esquina 100
Tu íntimo secreto 102
The Authors 105
Notes 113

ACKNOWLEDGEMENTS

This translation project owes a great debt of gratitude to the tango community in general, which is its primary audience as well as its main source of encouragement. Some of its dedicated members have played a more particular role in promoting my work along its way. I wish to thank Phil Jones and Maxfield Wollam-Fisher, producers of the weekly radio program *Bienvenidos al tango* on WOWD-LP Takoma Radio, for featuring my song translations on a weekly basis since the spring of 2020. I wish to thank Meredith Klein and the Philadelphia Argentine Tango School, for inviting me to share my work through several online lectures, and to the many participants who made those presentations so engaging with follow-up questions and side discussions. For her generous Foreword to this volume, and for sharing a decade of small research projects into tango lyrics and their cultural background, I wish to thank Beatriz Dujovne. For his help reviewing my prose here and for background research into song and music, I wish to thank Marty Demarest. And for her total support of my efforts in everything, on the dance floor as in our home life, I wish to thank Dasha Khripkova, to whom this volume is lovingly dedicated.

—AJS, 2022

FOREWORD

As a porteña who grew up listening to tangos being sung on the radio, I have always found literal translations a cacophony. They miss the point. For more than twenty years, I have read word-for-word translations of these songs—and grieved. My heart, already familiar with the glorious poetry of the tango, thus turns with relief to these lines Jake Spatz has given us, flowing smoothly and elegantly with the emotional sense of the porteño-Spanish originals. *Librotango* marks the debut of awesome tango lyrics in English.

Translating poetry isn't just about matching up two languages. There is a subculture of tango, within the culture of Buenos Aires, embedded in these lyrics, and an intimate knowledge of this world is mandatory for the task. In a sense, the translator has to be an ethnographer first, conducting fieldwork as a core part of the job. Spatz has been an ardent student of tango music and lyrics—of Argentine history, the record industry, and the artistic landscape of the Twentieth Century; of the theater, circus, opera, cinema—the true historical cradle where the tango developed. He knows this world. His translations are the fruit of two decades spent learning, absorbing, and living the tango.

Something new in Spatz's approach lies in his understanding of how the lyrics were actually written in the first place. More than anyone else to treat this subject in English, he has charted how the characters and images of one song appear in others, and how the tango was full of cross-references and borrowings from the very beginning. He is mapping out how the tango, in the shadow of the great opera houses of Buenos Aires, sprang to life as popular entertainment in plays and films drawing heavily on the dramas of the era, in the days long before record albums existed, when songs were made for stage and screen. Learning about the authors and their world has given him a perspective on how lyricists and composers treated tango as a collective fiction, quite literally a show they were all following while they were busy writing it. He has reached deeply into the careers of individual songwriters to learn their different styles, their ideas, even their collaborations. This vast thesis, this gestalt, gives his translations at once the detail of an academic compendium and the overall vision of a dramaturge.

This is what makes Spatz's work faithful instead of merely literal. He finds the right expression to capture and relay what the originals are actually *saying* and *doing* with their language. And to futher honor the poetry he so clearly loves, he adds the devotion of a scholar. Here is where Spatz puts on his ethnographer's hat and leaves no stone unturned. He consults old dictionaries and newspapers from the times when these lyrics were first created. He tracks down old scores and films, to place each song in its original context. He compares recordings, searching for variants in the lyrics. And besides all this, he interviews as many porteños as he can—myself happily among them—to investigate not just the words of these songs but their connotations. He is relentless. Accuracy is not enough for him; he goes the extra mile in search of consensus, the native audience's approval.

When it comes to the artistry that ties all this together to bring these songs into a new language, Spatz's work stands by itself. There is some challenging material in this first volume—"Mano a mano," "Cambalache," "Los mareados," "Tinta roja"—and I am in awe of how he makes their *lunfardo* slang and impressionism seem so natural in English. All this, too, while matching the original rhymes and rhythms, sometimes even their actual vowels, so that they can be performed with no change in melody.

The sense and the tone of these tangos is all here. This is their verbal music, their way of saying what they say. Very few bilingual and bicultural porteños could have done such a deed, and it is a good thing that this is only the first installment of the series. We want more.

—BEATRIZ DUJOVNE, author of
In Strangers' Arms: The magic of the tango

VOLUME ONE

INTRODUCTION

The tango is a three-minute opera... a sad thought you can dance to... a page torn out of an epic, that flaps away in the night on the wind of the docks...

Sentimental yet streetwise, soaring among the chandeliers, and yet grounded there in the mud beside the derricks and the oilcans, the tango embodies a clash of opposites. It speaks to man and to woman, to the homely and to the worldly; it sings of the present moment and of the past era; its greatest successes are pictures of the greatest failures. And the first enduring topic of this self-making urban mythology is the tango itself, so often playing in the background of the stories told in these songs, where streetlights glow in the mist and cobblestones glaze with tears; where the gray dawn rises over a world smeared by the grime of the machine age, with its pinstriped urbanity, its champagne-guzzling opportunism, and its glamourous corruption. The city of Buenos Aires looms large in these songs, as its people fight on the outskirts, love and grieve in the tenement courtyards, and smirk their way through the streets. The songs talk to each other, like neighbors chatting from their balconies, using an internal network of images and phrases—a kind of poetic jargon that runs deeper than any slang of the moment. The tango chronicles an ongoing drama full of recurring characters, telling their stories, showing glimpses of a saga.

What has become clear to me while studying and translating these lyrics is that their authors, the tango poets, were the first audience of this show. They were watching it as they were writing it, using the very plots and characters they saw before them. They crafted these tangos for the stage: there were no record albums back then, but there were dozens of one-acts opening every week, running for a fortnight, and closing to make room for others.

By the 1930s, these small-format shows were getting retailored to suit the new media of the day. Radio programs were now being broadcast to homes everywhere at once; sound movies, which the world was still learning how to produce, were opening in movie houses on different continents. All these venues needed material, and the theatrical world of the day was accelerating and diversifying to meet the demand—and a good song could sell an awful lot of tickets. Like Tin Pan Alley, it was all a veritable industry of song.

THEY CALL ME MILONGUITA

This popular culture of the day was entertainment's lower genre, as it were. All this bustle of activity and rapidity of songwriting and staging was going on in the shadow of the great opera houses: and no city in the Americas had as many opera houses, or such opulent ones, as the queen of the silver river, Buenos Aires.

The characters, situations, and themes of the early tango are largely borrowed from *verismo* operas, which were the biggest draw of the early 1900s—shows like *La Traviata*, *Manon*, and *La Bohème*. These depict the demimonde, the nightlife of casino and cabaret, where poor but talented young women could serve as playthings of the moneyed elite, as each party did its noble best to enjoy and exploit the other. Often we see the characters the morning after, in their moment of inwardness. Early tangos like "Zorro gris" and "Mano a mano" depict all this scenery transposed to the 1920s. "Milonguita," a formative tango quoted by numerous later songs, echoes a famous moment from *La Bohème*—"Now they call you Milonguita," says the flapper of herself, recalling the aria *Mi chiamano Mimì* ("They call me Mimí.") The tango "Griseta" even names the tragic heroines of the opera and theater, who were on everyone's mind at the time—Marguerite Gauthier, Mimí, Musetta, Manon... Later tangos name the fictional tango vixens, the flappers and singers, who were modeled on these icons—Estercita, Griseta, Malena...

This indebtedness of the tango to opera, so obvious once pointed out, is seldom mentioned nowadays, perhaps because tango lyrics are not often discussed on a deep level, as a literature. There is something else about these original plays, however, which has also gotten rather lost in history, and has led to some misunderstanding. Quite often, on the stage, in the skits for which these old tangos were written, the singer is not a man putting down a woman. As you can figure out from old synopses, and from the dedications on the sheet music for some of these songs, the singer was actually this female character, singing of herself in the third person, telling her own story. The character Milonguita is even named Ester in the song, after the actress who first portrayed her. Later eras have assumed that there was a chauvinism in these portrayals, a pejorative agenda projecting all these women of ill repute: but the truth is that popular song, generally speaking, was less chauvinistic then than it is now. When the tangos were born in the spotlights of little theaters, sometimes the fallen heroine, the fiction on loan from the opera next door, was the one telling her own story, speaking her own real name.

The opera also gave the tango its characteristic style of singing. There is no greater real-life figure in the tango than Carlos Gardel, the charismatic singer, and actor, and composer, whose life was cut short by a plane crash in 1935, but who left a large legacy of recordings. Not only does he sing better every day, as the saying goes, but he taught the world how to sing a tango. Gardel's way of singing was emotive, voice straining under the pressure of feeling within, sometimes almost breaking into a sob. Gardel learned that style, which he mastered with a unique charm, from the biggest opera tenor of the day, one of the two or three greatest of the Twentieth Century: the searingly dramatic Enrico Caruso, who would often break the composure of perfection by pushing a sob or a cry into his voice, to thrilling effect.

Yet the tango, with its rapidly developing songbook of lyrics, was not just a street opera, and not just a music hall spectacle of popular appeal. There is one other major influence which, like the opera, was widespread in the culture at the time, and which was newly shaping the psychology of the people. The inwardness in tango lyrics, the comfort with mixed feelings and ambivalence, the irony about desire and defeat—these are the moods of a distinctly Freudian consciousness.

TELL ME ABOUT YOUR BARRIO

Freud's impact on everyday life in Argentina was immense. Since the early 1900s, psychotherapy has remained a normal part of city life. Coming to grips with the tragedies of experience, and delving down into vulnerability to regain one's sanity, are Freudian attitudes. So is the emotional honesty one finds in many tangos, whenever someone wants to hide in self-deception, or spit out the truth at all costs, or pursue the obsession with naming things like people and places, a motif which appears quite often. Where the Freudian influence appears in jazz songs, it is usually there for comedy's sake; but in the tango it is a way of being, a way of confronting and yet embracing the uncertainty and anxiety of life in the modern world.

This sensibility also explains what is really going on in many tangos that give voice to darker emotions. At first they may seem like they're wallowing in guilt and regret. Under finer consideration, however—for let us be connoisseurs of the deeps—these are also moments of recognition, songs of conscience. The blues, too, sings of the down and out, but in the tango there is also a sense of returning to the repressed, of speaking a truth avoided before. There is not just a sadness but the narrative of its discovery and the trial of naming it.

There is also a certain affinity for impressionism, especially as the tango songbook develops and begins adopting a new aesthetic early in the 1940s. Free association, a heap of poetic details, suddenly becomes a new kind of tango lyric, as in "Tinta roja"; words and images from other songs suddenly retell old stories from new perspectives, as when "Percal" retells "Milonguita." And these are *dance tunes.*

Yet as Freud himself said of his work, the poets were there first.

Here, then, are the combining clash of opera and psychoanalysis, of champagne and the mud, of the starlet and the varlet, of the mist of the past and the clarity of memory's half-light. Here are the poets of the book of the tango.

—AJS, 2021

VOLUME ONE

A NOTE ON THE TEXT

My arrangement of these texts departs in some cases from their printings in the sheet music (which itself can vary between editions). My goal with this is twofold: first, to undo some obvious compromises and errors, brought about by printing the song lyrics at the bottom of a musical score; secondly, to reveal the underlying poetic form of the lyrics, which is more regular than the sheet music sometimes suggests. Besides making the lyrics more suitable for book layout, this additionally serves to make them more coherent, by not overly atomizing them, and by letting them breathe in their rhythms more naturally. It's a little like fine-tuning a radio to get a clearer signal.

RHYTHM AND FORM

The melodic unit in these songs is usually a phrase of eight downbeats. These phrases, or long lines of verse, usually break into two, three, or four line segments (hemistichs), depending on the rhythm and tempo of the vocal delivery. My graphic rearrangement of the lyrics has made this structure more consistent throughout the book, without denying the various songs a certain flexibility of treatment.

For every four musical downbeats (quarter notes), one may usually count eight metrical or prosodic beats (eighth notes), since the poetic beat includes the upbeat of the music. Stronger verbal stresses land on the downbeat, as shown in these lines from "Tu íntimo secreto":

> La dicha es un castillo con un puente de cristal,
> camina suavemente si lo quieres alcanzar.

> True | bliss is like a castle with a | bridge made out of glass, ( )
> Go walking ever softly if you wish to safely pass.

Each line has four downbeats, as indicated. By traditional poetic scansion, there are eight prosodic beats (including a rest at the end), as shown by the accent marks above the first line of the English version, which also diagrams two measures of music in 2/4 time. My translation strives to be singable, and to follow the rhythm and melody of the originals, so I have taken care to shape my lines in this manner, following the music as closely as possible without violating prosodic patterning.

RHYME

Spanish prosody has different rules for rhyming than English does, and makes frequent use of assonance rhyme, where the vowels match but the terminal consonants do not (as in *cristal* and *alcanzar*, in the example above, or voz and *corazón*). This kind of rhyme is common in tangos, especially in the terminal position of the stanza (stanzas can also end without a rhyme).

Since it rhymes the vowel and ignores everything else, assonance rhyme appears prevalently in song lyrics in English already, especially in the blues tradition and genres influenced by it; but in literary verse it is usually considered faulty.

PRONUNCIATION

Lastly, the pronunciation of *castellano* (Spanish) in Argentina and Uruguay incorporates *sheísmo*, whereby the consonants *y* and *ll* (both make the same sound) are voiced *zh* or *sh*, as in the French *j* or the English words *measure* or *shine*. Thus the first person pronoun *yo*, for instance, is said *sho* or *zho*.

The *voseo* is also used informally, whereby the second person plural pronoun *vos* (you, Fr. *vous*, y'all) is used interchangeably with the singular *tú*, and is conjugated with a singular verb, as in the first line of "Milonguita," (vos eras = you was). In modern English, the *tú* form (thou) is obsolete, so we actually mirror the *voseo* already.

Librotango

· VOLUME 1 ·

MILONGUITA

SAMUEL LINNIG, 1920

VERSO 1

¿Te acordás, Milonguita? Vos eras
la pebeta más linda 'e Chiclana;
la pollera cortona y las trenzas,
y en las trenzas un beso de sol.
Y en aquellas noches de verano,
¿qué soñaba tu almita, mujer,
al oír en la esquina algún tango
chamuyarte bajito de amor?

ESTRIBILLO

Estercita,
hoy te llaman Milonguita,
flor de noche y de placer,
flor de lujo y cabaret.
Milonguita,
los hombres te han hecho mal
y hoy darías toda tu alma
por vestirte de percal.

VERSO 2

Cuando sales por la madrugada,
Milonguita, de aquel cabaret,
toda tu alma temblando de frío
dices: ¡Ay, si pudiera querer!...
Y entre el vino y el último tango
p'al cotorro te saca un bacán...
¡Ay, qué sola, Estercita, te sientes!
Si llorás... ¡dicen que es el champán!

MILONGUITA

SAMUEL LINNIG, 1920

VERSE 1

Do you recall, Milonguita? You once were
The prettiest girl of Chiclana;
With your bashful long skirts and your hair-braids,
And in your hair-braids, a kiss of the sun.
And during those evenings of summer,
What was your womanly soul dreaming of,
As you heard on the corner some tango
With its low, luring whispers of love?

CHORUS

Esthercita…
Now they call you Milonguita,
Flower of nightlife and play,
Of the luxury lounge cabaret.
Milonguita…
The men have treated you wrong,
And you'd give up your whole soul now
To put your percale back on.

VERSE 2

As you step in the dark of the morning,
Milonguita, from that cabaret,
With your whole soul a shiver of coldness,
You say, Ah, if love just came my way!…
And between the first wine and last tango,
Some tycoon takes you back to his place…
How alone, little Esther, you're feeling!
When you cry… they all blame the champagne!

MANO A MANO

CELEDONIO FLORES, 1923

VERSO 1

Rechiflado en mi tristeza, te evoco y veo que has sido
en mi pobre vida paria sólo una buena mujer.
Tu presencia de bacana puso calor en mi nido,
fuiste buena, consecuente, y yo sé que me has querido
como no quisiste a nadie, como no podrás querer…

ESTRIBILLO 1

Se dio el juego de remanye cuando vos, pobre percanta,
gambeteabas la pobreza en la casa de pensión…
Hoy sos toda una bacana, la vida te ríe y canta,
los morlacos del otario los jugás a la marchanta
como juega el gato maula con el mísero ratón.

VERSO 2

Hoy tenés el mate lleno de infelices ilusiones,
te engrupieron los otarios, las amigas y el gavión;
la milonga, entre magnates, con sus locas tentaciones,
donde triunfan y claudican milongueras pretensiones,
se te ha entrado muy adentro en tu pobre corazón.

ESTRIBILLO 2

Nada debo agradecerte, mano a mano hemos quedado;
no me importa lo que has hecho, lo que hacés ni lo que harás…
Los favores recibidos creo habértelos pagado
y, si alguna deuda chica sin querer se me ha olvidado,
en la cuenta del otario que tenés se la cargás.

(Cont.)

FAIR AND SQUARE

CELEDONIO FLORES, 1923

VERSE 1

Going crackers in my sadness, I get thinking back upon you,
And in my poor pariah life, how good a woman you had been.
With your little flapper airs you made my nest the brighter too,
You were good to me, accountable, and I know you loved me true
Like you'd never loved another, like you'll never love again…

CHORUS 1

The guessing game was up when you were just a poor young doll
Giving poverty the slip back in the shabby boarding house…
Now life's a laugh and song to you, the made girl standing tall,
And you throw your daddy's ducats round, content to play the moll
Like a crafty kitten toying with a miserable mouse.

VERSE 2

Today your bonnet's all abuzz with madcap expectations,
Your girlfriends, chumps, and romeos just take you for a ride;
The nightclub, with its millionaires and all its mad temptations,
With its jackpots and its washing out of flapper aspirations,
Keeps tugging at your poor girl's little heart from deep inside.

CHORUS 2

I've not a scrap to thank you for, fair and square we ended;
I don't mind what you've done, or what you're doing, or shall do…
I believe I've paid you back for any favors you extended,
And if some little debt has gone forgotten, unintended,
Just charge it to that chump's account next time the bill is due.

(Cont.)

VERSO 3

Mientras tanto, que tus triunfos, pobres triunfos pasajeros,
sean una larga fila de riquezas y placer;
que el bacán que te acamala tenga pesos duraderos,
que te abrás de las paradas con cafishos milongueros
y que digan los muchachos: Es una buena mujer.

ESTRIBILLO 3

Y mañana, cuando seas descolado mueble viejo
y no tengas esperanzas en tu pobre corazón,
si precisás una ayuda, si te hace falta un consejo,
acordate de este amigo que ha de jugarse el pellejo
pa'ayudarte en lo que pueda cuando llegue la ocasión.

VERSE 3

Meanwhile, may your winnings, your poor momentary winnings,
Be a steady string of riches and a boisterous bacchanale…
May the bigshot who supports you never see his bankroll thinning,
May the pushers in the nightclubs ever greet you with a grinning,
And the fellas say about you: Now there goes a decent gal.

CHORUS 3

And tomorrow, when you hit the curb like last year's decorations,
And your poor old heart is left without a hope, without a dime,
If you need a helping hand, or if you're short on information,
You recall your pal who'd risk his skin without one hesitation
To help you out as best he can, whenever comes the time.

CAMINITO

GABINO CORIA PEÑALOZA, 1926

VERSO 1

Caminito que el tiempo ha borrado
que juntos un día nos viste pasar,
he venido por última vez,
he venido a contarte mi mal.
Caminito que entonces estabas
bordeado de trébol y juncos en flor,
una sombra ya pronto serás,
una sombra lo mismo que yo.

ESTRIBILLO

Desde que se fue,
triste vivo yo;
caminito amigo,
yo también me voy.
Desde que se fue
nunca más volvió.
Seguiré sus pasos,
caminito, adiós.

VERSO 2

Caminito que todas las tardes
feliz recorría cantando mi amor,
no le digas si vuelve a pasar
que mi llanto tu suelo regó.
Caminito cubierto de cardos,
la mano del tiempo tu huella borró;
yo a tu lado quisiera caer
y que el tiempo nos mate a los dos.

LITTLE PATHWAY

GABINO CORIA PEÑALOZA, 1926

VERSE 1

Little pathway that time now has faded,
That once saw together the two of us go—
I've come back to you one last time,
I've come back here to tell you my woes.
Little pathway that once was embroidered
All over with clover and flowering reeds—
You will just be a shadow here soon,
Just a shadow, the same way as me.

CHORUS

Since she went away,
All I've done is cry;
Little pathway, my fellow,
Now it's my time to go.
Since she went away,
She never came back, no...
Now I follow her footsteps,
Fare you well, little road.

VERSE 2

Little pathway that once in the evenings
I used to run lightsomely, singing of love,
Never tell her, if ever she's here,
How your surface ran wet with my tears.
Little pathway now choked up with thistles,
Time's hand has erased where you go...
Would that I too might fall at your side,
And we both could be slain by the years.

ALMA EN PENA

FRANCISCO GARCÍA JIMÉNEZ, 1928

VERSO 1

Aún el tiempo no logró
llevar su recuerdo,
borrar las ternuras
que guardan escritas
sus cartas marchitas
que tantas lecturas
con llanto desteñí…
¡Ella sí que me olvidó!…
Y hoy frente a su puerta
la oigo contenta,
percibo sus risas,
y escucho que a otro
le dice las mismas
mentiras que a mí…

ESTRIBILLO

Alma… que en pena vas errando,
acércate a su puerta
suplícale llorando:
Oye… perdona si te pido
mendrugos del olvido
que alegre te hace ser…
¡Tú me enseñaste a querer, y he sabido!
Y haberlo aprendido
de amores me mata…
Y yo que voy aprendiendo hasta a odiarte,
tan sólo a olvidarte
no puedo aprender!…

(Cont.)

SOUL IN SORROW

FRANCISCO GARCÍA JIMÉNEZ, 1928

VERSE 1

Even time was of no use
At fading her memory,
At stopping the smiting
Of seeing her writing
In letters that withered
From so many readings
With tears falling free…
She moved on and cut me loose!
And now by her doorway
I hear her contented,
Catch wind of her laughter,
And hark to her telling
Some other the same lies
She once told to me…

CHORUS

Soul… as in sorrow you go straying,
Draw closer to her doorway,
Shedding tears and saying:
Hey there… pardon me for begging
A crust of that forgetting
That leaves you glad and whole…
You taught me well in the fine art of yearning!
And now by my learning,
My love will undo me…
I'm even learning by now to regret you,
Since how to forget you
Was lost on my soul!…

(Cont.)

VERSO 2

Esa voz que vuelvo a oír,
un día fué mía,
y hoy de ella es apenas
el eco el que alumbra
mi pobre alma en pena,
que cae moribunda
al pie de su balcón…
Esa voz que maldecí,
hoy oigo que a otro
promete la gloria,
y cierro los ojos,
y es una limosna
de amor, que recojo
con mi corazón…

VERSE 2

That same voice I hear again,
Was one day my darling's,
And now it is solely
The echo that reaches
My poor soul in sorrow,
Which under her window
Sinks down to depart…
That same voice I cursed back when
I hear give some other
The promise of glory
Which, with my eyes shutting,
Is love's little handout,
Which I lie accepting
With all of my heart…

MADRESELVA

LUIS CÉSAR AMADORI, 1931

VERSO 1

Vieja pared
del arrabal,
tu sombra fué
mi compañera.
De mi niñez
sin esplendor
la amiga fué
tu madreselva.
Cuando, temblando,
mi amor primero,
con su esperanza
besó mi alma,
yo, junto a vos,
pura y feliz,
cantaba así
mi primera confesión:

ESTRIBILLO 1

Madreselvas en flor, que me vieron nacer,
y en la vieja pared sorprendieron mi amor…
Tu humilde caricia es como el cariño
primero y querido que siento por él!
Madreselvas en flor, que trepándose van,
es tu abrazo tenaz y dulzón como aquel…
Si todos los años tus flores renacen
hacé que no muera mi primer amor!

(Cont.)

HONEYSUCKLE

LUIS CÉSAR AMADORI, 1931

VERSE 1

Old boundary wall
Around the slums,
Your shadow once
Was my companion.
When I was young,
And all was drab,
I found my friend
Your honeysuckle.
When, all atremble,
My very first love
Left on my soul there
The kiss of hoping,
There at your side,
All glad and pure,
I sang the song
Of my first confession so:

CHORUS 1

Honeysuckle in bloom, you saw when I was born,
And along the old wall listened in on my love:
Your humble caresses are like that affection,
The first and the warmest I felt in my heart!
Honeysuckle in bloom, that goes climbing along,
Your embrace is as strong and as sweet as his own…
If year after year now, your flowers reopen,
May never my first love thus come to an end!

(Cont.)

PUENTE

Pasaron los años,
y mis desengaños
yo vengo a contarte,
mi vieja pared…

VERSO 2

Así aprendí
que hay qué fingir
para vivir
decentemente.
Que amor y fe
mentiras son,
y del dolor
se ríe la gente.
Hoy que la vida
me ha castigado
y me ha enseñado
su credo amargo,
vieja pared,
con emoción
me acerco a vos,
y te digo como ayer:

ESTRIBILLO 2

Madreselvas en flor, que me vieron nacer,
y en la vieja pared sorprendieron mi amor:
tu humilde caricia es como el cariño
primero y querido que nunca olvidé.
Madreselvas en flor, que trepandose van,
es tu abrazo tenaz y dulzón como aquel.
Si todos los años tus flores renacen
porque ya no vuelve mi primer amor…

BRIDGE

Years have gone by now,
And opened my eyes now…
I'm back here to tell you,
My old boundary wall…

VERSE 2

I've come to learn
You must pretend
To live the good life
Forever after.
That love and faith
Are merely lies,
And sorrow meets
With people's laughter.
And now that real life
Has tricked and fooled me,
And ever schooled me
In its bitter teaching,
Old boundary wall,
With brimming heart,
I come to you,
And confide like yesterday:

CHORUS 2

Honeysuckle in bloom, you saw when I was born,
And across the old wall listened in on my love:
Your humble caresses are like that affection,
The first and the warmest, I'll never forget!
Honeysuckle in bloom, that goes climbing along,
Your embrace is as strong and as sweet as his own…
If year after year now, your flowers reopen,
Why cannot my first love come ever again…

CAMBALACHE

ENRIQUE SANTOS DISCÉPOLO, 1934

VERSO 1

Que el mundo fue y será
una porquería ya lo sé…
(¡en el quinientos seis
y en el dos mil también!)
Que siempre ha habido chorros,
maquiavelos y estafaos,
contentos y amargaos,
valores y dublé…
Pero que el siglo veinte es un despliegue
de maldá insolente,
ya no hay quien lo niegue.
Vivimos revolcaos en un merengue
y en un mismo lodo
todos manoseaos…

ESTRIBILLO 1

¡Hoy resulta que es lo mismo
ser derecho que traidor!…
¡ignorante, sabio o chorro,
generoso o estafador!
¡Todo es igual! ¡Nada es mejor!
¡Lo mismo un burro que un gran profesor!
No hay aplazaos ni escalafón,
los inmorales nos han igualao.
Si uno vive en la impostura
y otro roba en su ambición,
¡Da lo mismo que sea cura,
colchonero, rey de bastos,
caradura o polizón!…

(Cont.)

HOCKSHOP

ENRIQUE SANTOS DISCÉPOLO, 1934

VERSE 1

That the world has been and will always be
A pigsty, that I knew…
(And in Fourteen-Ninety-Two
And Two Thousand all the same!)
That it's always been a den of thieves
And dupes and Machiavels,
Well-offs and ne'er-do-wells,
Genuines and fakes…
But that the Twentieth Century is a riot
Of absolute skulduggery,
There's no one who'd deny it!
We all live rolling round in one molasses,
And in one muck together,
Grope each other down…

CHORUS 1

Today it all turns out the same
To be faithful or a façade,
A wise guy, dunce, or copycat,
Philanthropist or fraud!
All fare the same!… Nobody's better!
A horse's ass rivals a great old professor!
No one can fail, no one excels,
Those with no morals have evened the scales.
If this one's life is all imposture
And that one steals another's pay,
They're just like one who takes the tonsure,
A couch potato, a king of clubs,
A spoiled brat or stowaway!…

(Cont.)

VERSO 2

¡Qué falta de respeto,
qué atropello a la razón!
¡Cualquiera es un señor!
¡Cualquiera es un ladrón!
Mezclao con Stavisky va
Don Bosco y "La Mignón",
Don Chicho y Napoleón,
Carnera y San Martín…
Igual que en la vidriera irrespetuosa
de los cambalaches,
se ha mezclao la vida,
Y herida por un sable sin remaches
ves llorar la Biblia
contra un calefón…

ESTRIBILLO 2

¡Siglo veinte, cambalache
problemático y febril!…
El que no llora no mama
y el que no afana es un gil!
¡Dale nomás! ¡Dale que va!¡
que allá en el horno nos vamo a encontrar!
¡No pienses más, sentate a un lao,
que a nadie importa si naciste honrao!
Es lo mismo el que labura
noche y día como un buey,
Que el que vive de los otros,
que el que mata, que el que cura
o está fuera de la ley…

VERSE 2

What disrespect for decency,
What a trampling on the books!
Now everyone's a gentle sir!
Now everyone's a crook!
All mixed up with Stavisky goes
Don Bosco and "The Tart,"
Don Chicho and Bonaparte,
Carnera and San Martín…
The same way, in the heartless hockshop window,
You see life's shuffled stages
In bric-a-brac disorder,
And wounded by a hanger through the pages,
Against the water heater,
The Bible hangs in tears…

CHORUS 2

Fevered, shaky Twentieth Century—
Hockshop fit to collapse!
You squeal or you don't suckle,
And everyone pinches but saps!
Go right ahead! Just have a go!
We'll all meet again in the furnace below!
Don't think it through, just step aside,
Nobody cares you were born dignified!
It makes no difference if you labor
Like a packmule dusk to dawn,
Or if you're sponging off of others,
Or you're a killer, or a savior,
Or you live outside the law…

NO ME PREGUNTEN POR QUÉ

REINALDO PIGNATARO, 1935

VERSO 1

¡Muchachos!…
Si cualquiera de estas noches
me ven llegar al café,
tambaleando medio "colo"
babeando y hablando solo,
¡no me pregunten por qué!
Borracho…
Con la melena revuelta,
la corbata floja y suelta
y con rencor al mirar,
no me pregunten, muchachos,
por qué he venido borracho
y de mi tengan piedad.

ESTRIBILLO

En la luz de unos ojos divinos
se embriagaban mi alma y mi fe
y en la copa de miel de sus labios
hasta ayer de pasión me embriagué.
Hoy que vivo de nuevo en tinieblas
añorando la luz de su amor
necesito hundir mi existencia
y es por eso que busco el alcohol.

(Cont.)

DON'T GO ASKING ME WHY

REINALDO PIGNATARO, 1935

VERSE 1

My buddies!...
If on any of these evenings
You see me coming in the bar,
With a stumble, off my rocker,
Just a drooling, solo talker,
Don't go asking me why!
All drunken...
With my hairdo all disheveled,
And my crooked tie bedeviled,
And a rancor in my eyes,
Don't go asking me, buddies,
Why I've come in so drunken,
And show some mercy instead.

CHORUS

In the light of those eyes shining holy
Were enraptured my soul and my faith,
On the cup of those lips full of honey
I was passion-drunk through yesterday.
Now I'm living and yearning in darkness
For that light of her love above all,
Now I need to submerge my existence
And that's why I seek out alcohol.

(Cont.)

VERSO 2

¡Muchachos!…
Si cualquiera de estas noches
me ven llegar al café
tambaleando medio "colo"
babeando y hablando solo
¡no me pregunten por qué!
Borracho…
Refugiado en el alivio
del brebaje dulce y tibio
que nos prodiga el licor,
tal vez me olvide de aquella
que hasta ayer fuera mi estrella
y hoy me mata de dolor.

VERSE 2

My buddies!...
If on any of these evenings
You see me coming in the bar,
With a stumble, off my rocker,
Just a drooling, solo talker,
Don't go asking me why!
All drunken...
Seeking refuge in the brews
That the sweet and mellow booze
All so lavishly bestows,
Perhaps I might forget the way
She was my polestar yesterday
And now kills me with woe.

EL DÍA QUE ME QUIERAS

ALFREDO LE PERA, 1935

VERSO 1

Acaricia mi ensueño
el suave murmullo
de tu suspirar.
Como rie la vida
si tus ojos negros
me quieren mirar.
Y si es mio el amparo
de tu risa leve
que es como un cantar,
ella aquieta mi herida,
todo, todo se olvida.

ESTRIBILLO 1

El día que me quieras
la rosa que engalana,
se vestirá de fiesta
con su mejor color.
Y al viento las campanas
dirán que ya eres mía,
y locas las fontanas
se contaran su amor.

(Cont.)

THE DAY YOU EVER LOVE ME

ALFREDO LE PERA, 1935

VERSE 1

It's toying with my daydreams,
That gentle little music
That murmurs in your sighs…
What's life made of but laughter
When you show me all the darkling
Attention of your eyes!
And when I find my haven
Within your little chuckle
That's like a lullaby—
Then all the pains that grind me,
They're hushed and left behind me…

CHORUS 1

The day you ever love me,
The beautifying roses
Shall dress for celebration
And show their deepest hue.
And with the breezes blowing
The bells will say you're mine now,
And in love the fountains flowing
Shall all be crazy too.

(Cont.)

ESTRIBILLO 2

La noche que me quieras
desde el azul del cielo,
las estrellas celosas
nos mirarán pasar.
Y un rayo misterioso
hara nido en tu pelo,
luciernagas curiosas que veran
que eres mi consuelo.

VERSO 2

RECITADO

El día que me quieras
no habra más que armonía.
Será clara la aurora
y alegre el manantial.
Traerá quieta la brisa
rumor de melodía.
Y nos daran las fuentes
su canto de cristal.
El día que me quieras
endulzara sus cuerdas
el pajaro cantor.
Florecerá la vida,
no existira el dolor.

ESTRIBILLO 2

La noche que me quieras
desde el azul del cielo,
las estrellas celosas
nos mirarán pasar.
Y un rayo misterioso
hara nido en tu pelo,
luciernagas curiosas que veran
que eres mi consuelo.

CHORUS 2

The night you ever love me,
From in the blue of heaven
The stars will shine with envy
To watch us passing by.
And the mystery of a moonbeam
Shall nestle in your hair,
Curious fireflies shall all come out to see
You're the answer to my prayer.

VERSE 2

SPOKEN

The day you ever love me
There will be nothing but harmony.
The dawn shall brighten clear
And happy run the springs.
The quiet breeze shall bear us
Murmurs of a melody.
And crystal shall the water
Hail us as it sings.
The day you ever love me
The songbird shall be warbling
Softer than before.
Life shall break into flower,
Sorrow shall be no more.

CHORUS 2

The night you ever love me,
From in the blue of heaven
The stars will shine with envy
To watch us passing by.
And the mystery of a moonbeam
Shall nestle in your hair,
Curious fireflies shall all come out to see
You're the answer to my prayer.

ALMA DEL BANDONEÓN

DISCÉPOLO Y AMADORI, 1935

VERSO 1

Yo me burlé de vos
porque no te entendí
ni comprendí tu dolor.
Tuve la sensación
de que tu canto cruel
lo habías robao, bandoneón…
Recién comprendo bien
la desesperación
que te revuelve al gemir
¡Sos una oruga que quiso ser
mariposa antes de morir!

ESTRIBILLO

Fue tu voz, bandoneón,
la que me confió
el dolor del fracaso
que hay en tu gemir;
voz que es fondo de la vida
oscura y sin perdón,
del que soñó volar
y arrastra su ilusión
llorándola…

(Cont.)

SOUL OF THE BANDONEÓN

DISCÉPOLO & AMADORI, 1935

VERSE 1

I once made fun of you,
Because I never knew
Nor comprehended your woes.
I thought that all along
You stole your cruel song
From someone else, bandoneón…
Just now I understand
How that despairing groan
Goes ever stirring in you—
A caterpillar who wished to be
A butterfly before he was through!

CHORUS

By your moan, bandoneón,
There was told to me
All the woes of defeat there
Groaning as you breathe;
Moan from down where life is led
Obscure and never spared,
Who dreamt of flying free,
And drag your hope aground,
Despairingly…

(Cont.)

VERSO 2

Igual que vos soñé…
Igual que vos viví
sin alcanzar mi ambición.
Alma de bandoneón
—alma que arrastro en mí—
voz de desdicha y de amor,
te buscaré al morir,
te llamaré en mi adiós,
para pedirte perdón,
y al apretarte en mis brazos,
darte en pedazos
mi corazón.

VERSE 2

Like you I had a dream…
Like you I lived my life
Without achieving my goal.
Bandoneón, your soul
—The soul I drag in me—
Voice of despond and of love:
I'll seek you when I die,
I'll send you my goodbye
To beg forgiveness of you,
And with the tightest of squeezes,
Will break you the pieces
Of my own heart too.

NOSTALGIAS

ENRIQUE CADÍCAMO, 1936

VERSO 1

Quiero emborrachar mi corazón
para apagar un loco amor
que más que amor es un sufrir...
Y aquí vengo para eso,
a borrar antiguos besos
en los besos de otras bocas...
Si su amor fue "flor de un día"
¿porqué causa es siempre mía
esa cruel preocupación?
Quiero por los dos mi copa alzar
para olvidar mi obstinación
y más la vuelvo a recordar.

ESTRIBILLO

Nostalgias...
de escuchar su risa loca
y sentir junto a mi boca
como un fuego su respiración.
Angustia...
de sentirme abandonado
y pensar que otro a su lado
pronto... pronto le hablará de amor...
¡Hermano!...
Yo no quiero rebajarme,
ni pedirle, ni llorarle,
ni decirle que no puedo más vivir...
Desde mi triste soledad veré caer
las rosas muertas de mi juventud.

(Cont.)

NOSTALGIAS

ENRIQUE CADÍCAMO, 1936

VERSE 1

I want to get my heart completely drunk
And put to rest a crazy love
Which more than love is pain I feel…
And that's the reason why I'm here,
So I can wipe old kisses clear
Upon the muzzle of the bottle…
If her love "blossomed but a day,"
Why can I never get away
From this cruel worry on my mind?
For both of us I want to lift a glass
To leave my stubbornness behind—
And only think of her the more.

CHORUS

Nostalgias…
For how her crazy laugher sounded,
How I felt my mouth surrounded
By the fire of the way that she breathed…
The anguish…
To feel abandoned and denied,
And think some other at her side
Will, any moment, be speaking of love…
My brother!…
I don't want to stoop before her,
Or to whimper, or implore her,
Or to tell her that no more… can I go on…
From in my saddened solitude, I'll watch them fall,
The withered roses that were once my youth.

(Cont.)

VERSO 2

Gime, bandoneón, tu tango gris,
quizá a ti te hiera igual
algún amor sentimental...
Llora mi alma de fantoche
sola y triste en esta noche,
noche negra y sin estrellas...
Si las copas traen consuelo
aquí estoy con mi desvelo
para ahogarlos de una vez...
Quiero emborrachar mi corazón
para después poder brindar
"por los fracasos del amor"...

VERSE 2

Cry, bandoneón, your tango gray,
Perhaps your heart is breaking too
For some old love that wounded you…
The puppet soul within me cries
Alone tonight, with saddened eyes,
Without a star, within the darkness…
If there's some solace in the drink,
Then here I stand, unslept a wink,
To drown them under, once for all…
I want to get my heart completely drunk
And once I'm ready, raise a toast:
"And here's to how love falls apart…"

QUIERO VERTE UNA VEZ MÁS

JOSÉ MARÍA CONTURSI, 1939

VERSO 1

Tarde que me invita a conversar
con los recuerdos…
pena de esperarte y de llorar
en este encierro!
Tanto en mi amargura te busque
sin encontrarte
cuando… cuando, vida, moriré
para olvidarte!

ESTRIBILLO

Quiero verte una vez más,
amada mia,
y extasiarme en el mirar
de tus pupilas!
Quiero verte una vez más,
aunque me digas
que ya todo terminó
y es inutil remover
las cenizas de un amor…
Quiero verte una vez más—
estoy tan triste!
y no puedo recordar
por que te fuiste…
Quiero verte una vez más,
y en mi agonia
un alivio sentiré
y olvidado en mi rincon
mas tranquilo moriré!

(Cont.)

I'VE GOT TO SEE YOU ONE MORE TIME

JOSÉ MARÍA CONTURSI, 1939

VERSE 1

Twilights always summon me to speak
With recollections...
I long for you with tears upon my cheek
In this dejection!
In bitterness I sought you far and wide
And never met you...
How much longer must I live, to die,
And so forget you!

CHORUS

I've got to see you one more time,
My lovely baby,
And see the pupils in your eyes
Still drive me crazy!
I've got to see you one more time,
Although you tell me
That it's all quite over now,
And it's useless poking round
In the ashes of a love...
I've got to see you one more time—
I live so sadly!
And I can't remember why
You left so madly...
I've got to see you one more time,
And in my anguish
Feel the tiniest allay,
And forgotten in my hole
All the calmer pass away!

(Cont.)

VERSO 2

Noche que consigues envolver
mis pensamientos…
Quejas que buscando nuestro ayer
las lleva el viento!
Sangre que ha vertido el corazón
al evocarte…
fiebre que me abrasa la razon
sin olvidarte!

VERSE 2

Night by night my memories of you
Close round me curling…
Moans that seek the yesterday we knew
The wind sets whirling…
Blood my heart was rushing at your name,
At having met you…
A fever sets my reason all aflame,
And can't forget you!

TINTA ROJA

CÁTULO CASTILLO, 1941

VERSO 1

Paredón…
tinta roja en el gris del ayer…
tu emoción de ladrillo feliz
sobre mi callejón
con un borrón
pintó la esquina…
Y al botón
que en el ancho de la noche
puso el filo de la ronda
como un broche…
Y aquel buzón carmín,
y aquel fondín
donde lloraba el tano
su rubio amor lejano
que mojaba con bon vin.

ESTRIBILLO

¿Dónde estará mi arrabal?
¿Quién se robó mi niñez?
¿En qué rincón, luna mía,
volcás como entonces
tu clara alegría?
Veredas que yo pisé,
malevos que ya no son,
bajo tu cielo de raso
trasnocha un pedazo
de mi corazón.

(Cont.)

RED INK

CÁTULO CASTILLO, 1941

VERSE 1

Boundary wall…
Your red ink in the gray of the past…
Your good mood with its brickwork of cheer…
Across my alley's blear,
With just one smear,
Drew all the corner…
And that patrol,
Who in the vastness of the night
Would shine the edges of his rounds
Just like a medal…
That pillar-box maroon—
And that old saloon
Where there wept the paisan
The far-off blonde he had his eyes on
And washed out in cheap wine.

CHORUS

Where did my old hood go?
Who stole my childhood away?
Within what corner, my moon,
Do you pour down clear joy
The way you used to?
The streets I used to stroll…
The hoodlums all long gone…
Beneath your open skies
A piece of my heart lies
From dark to dawn.

(Cont.)

VERSO 2

Paredón…
tinta roja en el gris del ayer…
borbotón de mi sangre infeliz
que vertí en el malvón
de aquel balcón
que la escondía…
Yo no sé
si fue negro de mis penas
o fue rojo de tus venas
mi sangría…
Por qué llegó y se fue
tras del carmín
y el gris fondín lejano
donde lloraba un tano
sus nostalgias de bon vin.

VERSE 2

Boundary wall…
Your red ink in the gray of the past…
And the spread of my blood in despair,
Which hit the window's red
Geranium bed
Where she retreated…
I don't know—
Was it the blackness of my pains,
Was it the red within your veins
That I was bleeding…
Why did she disappear,
Behind the old maroon,
And that far saloon's gray
Where a paisan washed away
His nostalgias in cheap wine.

QUÉ TE IMPORTA QUE TE LLORE

MIGUEL CALÓ & OSMAR MADERNA, 1942

VERSO 1

Déjame mentir que volverás
que volverás con el ayer,
con el ayer de nuestro sueño.
Déjame esperarte, ¡nada más!,
ya que comprendo que esperar
es un pedazo de recuerdo.
Se que este dolor
es el dolor de comprender
que no puede ser
esa esperanza que me ahoga.
Déjame llorar, siempre llorar,
y recordarte y esperar
al comprender que no volverás.

ESTRIBILLO

Qué te importa que te llore,
qué te importa que me mientas,
si ha quedado roto mi castillo del ayer,
déjeme hacer un Dios con sus pedazos.
Qué te importa lo que sufro,
qué te importa lo que lloro…
si no puede ser aquel ayer de la ilusión,
déjame así llorando nuestro amor.

(Cont.)

WHAT'S YOUR WORRY THAT I'M CRYING

MIGUEL CALÓ & OSMAR MADERNA, 1942

VERSE 1

Leave me here to lie that you'll return,
That you'll return with yesterday,
The yesterday we dreamt together…
Leave me here to—nothing more!—to yearn,
Now that I understand the way
That yearning's only recollection…
I know that all my grief
Is just the ache of finding out
The truth about my wish
Not coming true, and it destroys me…
Leave me crying, ever after crying,
And remembering you and trying
To understand you'll never come again…

CHORUS

What's your worry that I'm crying,
What's your worry I deceive me?
If all my castle walls of yesterday have tumbled down,
Then let me make a God from all the pieces!
What's your worry why I suffer,
What's your worry what I weep for…
If that old yesterday of all my dreams can never be,
Then leave me *me*, to cry for our love!

(Cont.)

VERSO 2

Mucho te esperé sin comprender,
sin comprender por qué razón
te has alejado y no volviste.
Mucho te esperé; fatal dolor
de consumir la soledad
en el calor de lo que fuiste.
Debes indicarme
qué camino continuar
ya que es imposible
que se junten nuestras vidas.
Déjame llorar, siempre llorar,
no ves que ya ni sé qué hablar,
ni qué mentir, ni qué esperar.

VERSE 2

Long I waited for you unaware,
All unaware of the reason why
You went away from me forever—
Long I waited for you, dead with grief
From spending all my time alone
To feel the warmth of what was over…
You have to tell me which
Among the pathways leads me on,
Now that it cannot be
That we can live our lives together…
Leave me crying, ever after crying—
You see I'm running out of words
And out of lies, and can't go wishing on!

MALENA

HOMERO MANZI, 1942

VERSO 1

Malena canta el tango como ninguna
y en cada verso pone su corazón.
A yuyo del suburbio su voz perfuma,
Malena tiene pena de bandoneón.
Tal vez allá en la infancia su voz de alondra
tomó ese tono oscuro de callejón,
o acaso aquel romance que sólo nombra
cuando se pone triste con el alcohol.
Malena canta el tango con voz de sombra,
Malena tiene pena de bandoneón.

ESTRIBILLO

Tu canción
tiene el frío del último encuentro.
Tu canción
se hace amarga en la sal del recuerdo.
Yo no sé
si tu voz es la flor de una pena,
Sólo sé
que al rumor de tus tangos, Malena,
te siento más buena, más buena que yo.

(Cont.)

MALENA

HOMERO MANZI, 1942

VERSE 1

Malena sings the tango like no one else does,
In every line she pours out a heart her own.
With grasses of the outskirts her voice is scented,
Malena knows the woes of the bandoneón.
Perhaps back in her childhood, her skylark singing
Took on the alley's darkened and dusky tone,
Or maybe it was that romance she never speaks of
Except within the sadness of drink alone.
Malena sings the tango with voice beshadowed,
Malena knows the woes of the bandoneón.

CHORUS

Through your song
Runs the chill of a final encounter.
Through your song
Stings the bitterest salt of remembering.
I don't know
If your voice rises out of a heartbreak,
All I know
Is at the quake of your tangos, Malena,
I feel that you're better, much better than me.

(Cont.)

VERSO 2

Tus ojos son oscuros como el olvido,
tus labios apretados como el rencor,
tus manos dos palomas que sienten frío,
tus venas tienen sangre de bandoneón.
Tus tangos son criaturas abandonadas
que cruzan sobre el barro del callejón,
cuando todas las puertas están cerradas
y ladran los fantasmas de la canción.
Malena canta el tango con voz quebrada,
Malena tiene pena de bandoneón.

VERSE 2

Your eyes are in a darkness of things forgotten,
Your lips contract with anger as white as bone,
Your hands are like two small doves that shake in coldness,
Your veins run with the blood of the bandoneón.
Your tangos are all creatures that run abandoned
Across the alleys' mud lanes they've always known,
When all the doors and houses are locked and shuttered
And phantoms in the songs raise a howling moan.
Malena sings the tango with voice all shattered,
Malena knows the woes of the bandoneón.

PEDACITO DE CIELO

HOMERO EXPÓSITO, 1942

VERSO 1

La casa tenía una reja
pintada con quejas
y cantos de amor;
La noche llenaba de ojeras
la reja, la hiedra
y el viejo balcón…
Recuerdo que entonces reías
si yo te leía
mi verso mejor,
y ahora, capricho del tiempo,
leyendo esos versos
¡lloramos los dos!

ESTRIBILLO

Los años de la infancia
¡pasaron!… ¡pasaron!…
La reja está dormida de tanto silencio…
y en aquel pedacito de cielo
se quedó tu alegría y mi amor.
Los años han pasado
¡terribles!… ¡malvados!…
dejando esa esperanza que no ha de llegar…
(¡Y recuerdo tu gesto travieso
después de aquel beso
robado al azar!…)

(Cont.)

SMALL PIECE OF HEAVEN

HOMERO EXPÓSITO, 1942

VERSE 1

The house had an old metal fencing
Awash with lamenting
And ballads of love;
The bruise of a shadow fell nightly
From fencing and ivy
And window above...
I think of how laughter would light you
When I would recite you
My greatest of rhymes,
And now, after time's own caprices,
To read those old verses
Brings tears to our eyes!

CHORUS

The season of our childhood
Has passed on... has passed on!...
The fencing lies asleep now, and silence has set in...
And there in that small piece of heaven
Remains your old cheer and my love.
The years have gone before us,
Unkindly... in horror!...
And they've left that old hope far behind...
(And I think back on your look of mischief
Right after that first kiss's
Stolen surprise!...)

(Cont.)

VERSO 2

Tal vez se enfrió con la brisa
tu cálida risa,
tu límpida voz…
Tal vez escapó a tus ojeras
la reja, la hiedra
y el viejo balcón…
Tus ojos de azúcar quemada
tenían distancias
doradas al sol…
¡Y hoy quieres hallar como entonces
la reja de bronce
temblando de amor!…

VERSE 2

The breeze perhaps chilled ever after
The warmth of your laughter,
The bell of your sighs…
Perhaps the old window, the ivy,
The fencing fled nightly
The bruise of your eyes…
Your eyes with their burnt sugar color
Receded to distances
Gold in the sun…
And now you would meet with old fondness
The old fence of bronze
All atremble with love!…

GRICEL

JOSÉ MARÍA CONTURSI, 1942

VERSO 1

No debi pensar jamás
en lograr tu corazón
y sin embargo te busqué
hasta que un día te encontré,
y con mis besos te aturdí
sin importarme que eras buena…
Tu ilusión fue de cristal,
se rompió cuando partí,
pues nunca, nunca más volví…
¡Que amarga fue tu pena!

ESTRIBILLO

"No te olvides de mi,
de tu Gricel,"
me dijiste al besar
el Cristo aquel,
y hoy que vivo enloquecido
porque no te olvidé
ni te acuerdas de mi,
¡Gricel, Gricel!

VERSO 2

Me faltó después tu voz
y el calor de tu mirar
y como un loco te busqué
pero ya nunca te encontré
y en otros besos me aturdí…
¡Mi vida toda fue un engaño!
¿Que será, Gricel, de mi?
Se cumplió la ley de Dios,
porque sus culpas ya pagó
quien te hizo tanto daño.

GRICEL

JOSÉ MARÍA CONTURSI, 1942

VERSE 1

Never should I once have thought
That I could have won your heart…
And still I sought you all the same,
Until I chanced on you one day,
And left you smitten by a kiss
Without a thought about your virtue!
All your hopes were crystal glass,
And shattered as I left you then,
To never, ever come again…
What bitter aching hurt you!

CHORUS

"Don't you stop thinking of me,
Of your Gricel,"
You implored me as you kissed
Your cross farewell—
And now I'm living driven crazy
Because I can't let you go…
And you don't remember me,
Gricel, Gricel!

VERSE 2

Soon I came to miss your voice
And the warmth within your eyes…
And looked for you as in a craze,
But never found you in my days,
And smitten by another's kiss…
Went living all my life untruly!
What shall come, Gricel, of me?
The laws of God were carried out,
Because I now have paid the cost
Of treating you so cruelly…

MAÑANA ZARPA UN BARCO

HOMERO MANZI, 1942

VERSO 1

Riberas que no cambian tocamos al anclar.
Cien puertos nos regalan la música del mar.
Muchachas de ojos tristes nos vienen a esperar
y el gusto de las copas parece siempre igual.
Tan solo aquí, en tu puerto, se alegra el corazón.
Riachuelo donde sangra la voz del bandoneón.
Bailemos hasta el eco del último compás,
mañana zarpa un barco, tal vez no vuelva más.

ESTRIBILLO

¡Qué bien se baila
sobre la tierra firme!
Mañana al alba
tenemos que zarpar.
La noche es larga,
no quiero que estés triste.
Muchacha, vamos,
no sé por qué llorás.
Diré tu nombre
cuando me encuentre lejos.
Tendré un recuerdo
para contarle al mar.
La noche es larga,
no quiero que estés triste.
Muchacha, vamos,
no sé por qué llorás.

(Cont.)

A SHIP SAILS OUT TOMORROW

HOMERO MANZI, 1942

VERSE 1

We touch down when we anchor on banks that never change.
A hundred ports regale us with music of the sea.
Girls come up to greet us with sadness in their eyes,
And the slug of every shot-glass always tastes the same.
Alone here, in your harbor, the heart discovers ease.
The bellows' voice bleeds over the Riachuelo's breeze.
Let's dance until the last beat has echoed to its end,
A ship sails out tomorrow, that may not come again.

CHORUS

How nice a feeling,
To dance on terra firma!
At dawn tomorrow,
We have to sail away.
The night's before us,
I want to see you happy.
Now come on, sweetheart,
What makes you want to cry?
I'll say your name there,
When faraway I find me.
I'll have a memory
To tell the rolling sea.
The night's before us,
I want to see you happy.
Now come on, sweetheart,
What makes you want to cry?

(Cont.)

VERSO 2

Dos meses en un barco viajó mi corazón.
Dos meses añorando la voz del bandoneón.
El tango es puerto amigo donde ancla la ilusión.
Al ritmo de su danza se hamaca la emoción.
De noche, con la luna, soñando sobre el mar
el ritmo de las olas me miente su compás.
Bailemos este tango, no quiero recordar.
Mañana zarpa un barco, tal vez no vuelva más.

VERSE 2

For two months on the ocean, my heart shipped out alone.
Two long months of missing the sounding bandoneón.
The tango is a harbor, where hopes at anchor ride.
In rhythm with its rocking, emotions sway inside.
At night, when there's a moon out, dreaming on the sea,
The rhythm of the waves feigns its measure to no end.
Let's dance away this tango, I don't want memories.
A ship sails out tomorrow, that may not come again.

ASÍ SE BAILA EL TANGO

MARVIL, 1942

VERSO 1

¡Qué saben los pitucos, lamidos y shushetas!
¡Qué saben lo que es tango, qué saben de compás!
Aquí está la elegancia. ¡Qué pinta! ¡Qué silueta!
¡Qué porte! ¡Qué arrogancia! ¡Qué clase pa' bailar!
Así se corta el césped mientras dibujo el ocho,
para estas filigranas yo soy como un pintor.
Ahora una corrida, una vuelta, una sentada…
¡Así se baila el tango, un tango de mi flor!

ESTRIBILLO

Así se baila el tango,
sintiendo en la cara,
la sangre que sube
a cada compás,
mientras el brazo,
como una serpiente,
se enrosca en el talle
que se va a quebrar.
Así se baila el tango,
mezclando el aliento,
cerrando los ojos
pa' escuchar mejor,
cómo los violines
le cuentan al fueye
por qué desde esa noche
Malena no cantó.

(Cont.)

THAT'S HOW YOU DANCE THE TANGO

MARVIL, 1942

VERSE 1

The ritzy, what do they know, the pretty boys and hipsters!
They haven't got the tango—its rhythm, not a chance!
Now, here is handsome for you. What style! What a figure!
What bearing! What audacity! What class it takes to dance!
That's how you cut the lawn up, while I'm designing the ocho,
I could have been a painter, for all these fancy lines.
Here comes a little quickstep, a pivot, and a sit-down…
That's how you dance the tango, a tango of my prime!

CHORUS

That's how you dance the tango,
Your hot face feeling
The blood come rising
With each beat's sound,
While just like a serpent
Your arm goes encircling
The waist of your partner
Who jackknifes around.
That's how you dance the tango,
Mixing your breathing,
Letting your eyes close
To take in the song,
To hear how the violins
Are telling the bellows
Malena stopped singing
From that night on.

(Cont.)

VERSO 2

¿Será mujer o junco, cuando hace una quebrada?
¿Tendrá resorte o cuerda para mover los pies?
Lo cierto es que mi prenda, que mi "peor es nada",
bailando es una fiera que me hace enloquecer...
A veces me pregunto si no será mi sombra
que siempre me persigue, o un ser sin voluntad.
¡Pero es que ya ha nacido así, pa' la milonga
y, como yo, se muere, se muere por bailar!

VERSE 2

Will it be a reed or woman, when breaking into poses?
Will there be springs or cables, to make her move her feet?
For certain it just grabs me, to me it's "better than nothing,"
Dancing is a frenzy and I'm crazy for the beat…
At times I even wonder if it shall be my shadow
Pursuing me forever, a thing some spell enchants.
That's just how it was born, then, to go to the milonga,
And just like me, it's dying, it's dying for a dance!

LOS MAREADOS

ENRIQUE CADÍCAMO, 1942

VERSO

Rara… como encendida
te hallé bebiendo linda y fatal…
Bebías y en el fragor del champán,
loca, reías por no llorar…
Pena… me dio encontrarte
pues al mirarte… yo vi brillar
tus ojos con un eléctrico ardor,
tus bellos ojos que tanto adoré…

ESTRIBILLO

Esta noche, amiga mía,
el alcohol nos ha embriagado…
¡Qué importa que se rían
y nos llamen los mareados!
Cada cual tiene sus penas
y nosotros las tenemos…
Esta noche beberemos
porque ya no volveremos
a vernos más…

TRIO

Hoy vas a entrar en mi pasado,
en el pasado de mi vida…
Tres cosas lleva mi alma herida:
amor… pesar… dolor…
Hoy vas a entrar en mi pasado
y hoy nuevas sendas tomaremos…
¡Qué grande ha sido nuestro amor!…
Y, sin embargo, ¡ay!,
mirá lo que quedó…

THE WASTED

ENRIQUE CADÍCAMO, 1942

VERSE

Weirdly… as in a spotlight,
I found you drinking, dressed up to die…
You drank there, and in the roar of champagne
Were laughing madly, so as not to cry…
Heartache… I felt to meet you,
And so to see you… to see in your eyes
The smoulder of an electrical warmth,
Within your dear eyes so deeply adored…

CHORUS

Here's to you, my old companion,
Booze tonight is all we've tasted…
What do I care if they're laughing
And guffawing that we're wasted…
Everybody has their sorrows,
We the same as any other…
Now tonight is ours to smother,
Since we'll never have another
To meet again…

TRIO

Now you must enter my past life,
The life I am leaving behind me…
Three things weigh my wounded mind:
Love… regret… and woe…
Now you must enter my past life,
And now we go our separate courses…
How mighty was the love we had before!
And now you see, alas,
The little left in store…

PERCAL

HOMERO EXPÓSITO, 1943

VERSO 1

Percal…
¿Te acuerdas del percal?
Tenias quince abriles,
anhelos de sufrir y amar,
De ir al centro, triunfar
y olvidar el percal.
Percal…
camino del percal,
Te fuiste de tu casa…
tal vez nos enteramos mal.
Sólo sé que al final
te olvidaste el percal.

ESTRIBILLO

La juventud se fue…
Tu casa ya no está…
Y en el ayer tirados
se han quedado
acobardados
tu percal y mi pasado.
La juventud se fue…
Yo ya no espero más…
Mejor dejar perdidos
los anhelos que no han sido
y el vestido de percal.

(Cont.)

PERCALE

HOMERO EXPÓSITO, 1943

VERSE 1

Percale…
Do you remember the percale?
You had fifteen Aprils in you,
A wish to suffer and to love,
To go downtown, and to prevail,
And leave behind the percale.
Percale…
The pathway of percale…
You ran away from home,
Perhaps we heard the story wrong.
I just know that in the end
You got away from the percale.

CHORUS

Now youth has gone away…
Your house is there no more…
And in that yesterday behind us
Lying cast aside,
All terrified,
Are your percale and my past life.
Now youth has gone away…
I hold out hopes no more…
It's best to leave as lost
The wish that never was
And the old dress of percale.

(Cont.)

VERSO 2

Llorar…
¿Por qué vas a llorar?…
¿Acaso no has vivido,
acaso no aprendiste a amar,
A sufrir, a esperar,
y también a callar?
Percal…
Son cosas del percal…
Saber que estás sufriendo
saber que sufrirás aún más
Y saber que al final
no olvidaste el percal.
Percal…
tristezas del percal.

VERSE 2

To cry…
What makes you want to cry?…
Did you somehow not live,
Did you not learn to love,
And to suffer, and to hope,
And then fall quiet too?
Percale…
They're just things of percale…
To know that now you suffer,
To know there's more ahead—
To know that in the end
You didn't leave the percale.
Percale…
The sorrows of percale.

ESTA NOCHE DE LUNA

HÉCTOR MARCÓ, 1943

VERSO 1

Acércate a mi
y oirás mi corazón:
contento latir como un brujo reloj…
La noche es azul;
convida a soñar…
Ya el cielo ha encendido su faro mejor.
Si un beso te doy…
pecado no ha de ser…
Culpable es la noche que incita a querer…
Me tienta el amor!
Acércate ya…
que el credo de un sueño nos redimirá…

PUENTE 1

Corre, corre, barcarola,
por mi río de ilusión:
que en el canto de las olas
surgirá mi confesión…

ESTRIBILLO

Soy… una estrella en el mar!
Que hoy detiene su andar
para hundirse en tus ojos…
Y en el embrujo
de tus labios muy rojos
por llegar a tu alma:
mi destino daré!…

(Cont.)

THIS NIGHT FULL OF MOONLIGHT

HÉCTOR MARCÓ, 1943

VERSE 1

Come closer to me,
And hear my heart dance,
As charmed as a clock in a sorcerer's trance…
The whole night is blue;
It leads one to dream…
Now the skies have enkindled their lantern supreme.
If I gave you a kiss…
A kiss were no sin…
It's just this encouraging night that we're in…
I'm tempted by love!
Draw close to me now…
By faith in a dream shall redemption be found…

BRIDGE 1

Hurry, hurry, barcarola,
Down my wishes' river run:
From the ballad of the waters
Shall my heart's confession come…

CHORUS

I… am a star on the sea!
That is slowing its speed
To sink down to your eyes now…
And in the witchcraft
Of the red of your smile,
To reach down to your soul,
I would give up my fate!

(Cont.)

ESTRIBILLO (CONT.)

Soy… una estrella en el mar!
Que hoy se pierde al azar
sin amor ni fortuna!
Y en los abismos
de esta noche de luna
sólo quiero vivir:
de rodilla a tus pies,
para amarte y morir!

VERSO 2

Acércate a mi
y oirás mi corazón
contento latir como un brujo reloj.
Mi voz te dirá
palabras de miel
que harán de tu pecho su fuego encender…
El canto del mar
repite en su rumor
qué noche de luna! qué noche de amor…
Dichoso de aquel
que pueda decir:
yo tengo un cariño, qué dulce es vivir!…

PUENTE 2

Corre, corre, barcarola,
que la luna se escondió.
Un amor llena la noche
y ese amor lo siento yo!

CHORUS (CONT.)

I… am a star on the sea!
Gone astray fancy-free
With no love, and no fortune!
And in the far deeps
Of this night full of moonlight,
All I want out of life
Is to kneel at your feet,
And to love you and die!

VERSE 2

Come closer to me,
And hear my heart dance,
As charmed as a clock in a sorcerer's trance.
I'll voice in your ear
Sweet words of desire
Whose warmth in your breast shall enkindle a fire…
The song of the sea
Keeps murmuring of
The night full of moonlight, the night full of love…
How blessed are those
Who are able to say:
What sweetness to live, with my love here to stay!

BRIDGE 2

Hurry, hurry, barcarola,
For the moon is now concealed.
Love is filling all the night in,
And that love is what I feel!

NADA

HORACIO SANGUINETTI, 1944

VERSO 1

He llegado hasta tu casa…
¡Yo no sé cómo he podido!
Si me han dicho que no estás,
que ya nunca volverás…
¡Si me han dicho que te has ido!
¡Cuánta nieve hay en mi alma!
¡Qué silencio hay en tu puerta!
Al llegar hasta el umbral,
un candado de dolor
me detuvo el corazón.

ESTRIBILLO

Nada, nada queda en tu casa natal…
Sólo telarañas que teje el yuyal.
El rosal tampoco existe y es seguro
que se ha muerto al irte tú…
¡Todo es una cruz!
Nada, nada más que tristeza y quietud…
Nadie que me diga si vives aún…
¿Dónde estás… para decirte
que hoy he vuelto arrepentido
a buscar tu amor?

VERSO 2

Ya me alejo de tu casa…
y me voy ya ni sé donde.
Sin querer te digo adiós
y hasta el eco de tu voz
de la nada me responde.
En la cruz de tu candado
por tu pena yo he rezado…
y ha rodado en tu portón
una lágrima hecha flor
de mi pobre corazón.

NOTHING

HORACIO SANGUINETTI, 1944

VERSE 1

Out I came to where your house is...
Who knows how I put the strength on!
If they had told me you're away,
To never come another day...
If they had told me that you're long gone!
My soul is under such a snowstorm!
Your door stands in such a silence!
And as I reached the entryway,
To see a padlock hanging there
Made my heart stop in despair.

CHORUS

Not a thing is left in your childhood home...
Only cobwebs weaving the brush overgrown.
The rambling rose no longer lives and when you left
It must have perished from the loss...
Everything's a cross!
Not a thing is here now but sadness and calm...
Not a soul to tell me if still you live on...
Where'd you go... for me to tell you
I've come back today repentant
To seek out your love?

VERSE 2

Off I go from where your house was...
And I'm heading I don't know where.
I bid goodbye without a choice,
And still the echo of your voice
Answers from the nothing in there.
On your padlock's crucifixion
I prayed for you in your affliction...
And there went rolling down your door
A tear become the finest flower
That my poor heart ever bore.

LLUEVE OTRA VEZ

OSCAR RUBENS, 1944

VERSO 1

Escucha… corazón…
el eco… de su voz…
Escucha, corazón, está lloviendo
y la lluvia va tejiendo
los recuerdos de su amor.
¡Qué pena… corazón!
No es ella… ni es su voz.
Tan sólo es la obsesión que me domina,
el recuerdo que castiga
desde su adiós.

ESTRIBILLO

Llueve… y un látigo de luz me azota,
relámpago de fiebre loca.
La lluvia, sin cesar,
golpeando en el cristal,
renueva la emoción perdida.
Y entre la bruma creo ver su imagen,
igual que entonces, diciendo adiós.
Llueve… y el cielo se llenó de sombras,
lo mismo que mi corazón.

VERSO 2

Tristeza… que dejó
el eco… de su voz.
Tristeza de esperar inútilmente
y creer que nuevamente
con la lluvia volverá.
¡No esperes… corazón!
¡No penes… por su amor!
Mañana cuando el sol radiante asome
al calor de otros amores,
olvidarás.

RAIN FALLS ONCE AGAIN

OSCAR RUBENS, 1944

VERSE 1

Listen… how, my heart…
The echo… of her sigh…
Listen how, my heart, the rainy weather
Goes weaving back together
The memories of her love.
A pity… how, my heart!
It's not her… it's not her sigh.
It's only this obsession that enslaves me,
The memory that flays me
Since her goodbye.

CHORUS

Rain falls… and the whips of light go lashing,
A crazy fever's lightning flashing.
This rain that will not pass
Goes drumming on the glass,
And dredges up a lost emotion.
And in the fog I seem to see her standing,
The same as back then, to say goodbye.
Rain falls… and the sky's aswarm with shadows,
The same as in this heart of mine.

VERSE 2

The sorrows… that left behind…
The echo… of her voice.
The sorrows of awaiting all in vain
And believing in the rain
To bring her back again.
Stop waiting… now, my heart!
Stop pining… for her love!
Tomorrow when the shining sun appears
Other loves will dry your tears,
And you'll move on.

GARRAS

JOSÉ MARÍA CONTURSI, 1945

VERSO 1

Callejón sin luz… esperándote…
Frío… sombras!
Ansias de vivir para tu amor
y no poder…
Siento que la vida se me vá… y no me lloras.
Busco desolado tu calor… y aquí no estás!
Agonía cruel… luego soledad
Y después tu olvido ¡nada más!

ESTRIBILLO

No pude más… y en mi afán por llegar
era un duende errabundo
que se perdió sin poderte encontrar
por las calles del mundo…
Y me he quedado como un pájaro sin nido…
como un niño abandonado…
con mis penas que se agarran como garras
y desgarran a mi corazón!

VERSO 2

Callejón sin luz… noche sin final…
Sombras… frío!
Gracias por venir con tu perdón
y tu bondad…
Ya mi pobre vida terminó… y estoy vacío,
Muerto para el mundo y para vos mi corazón!
Agonía cruel… luego soledad
Este llanto tuyo y ¡nada más!

CLAWS

JOSÉ MARÍA CONTURSI, 1945

VERSE 1

Alley in the dark… waiting still for you…
Coldness… shadows!
Anxious to live life just for your love…
Unable to…
I feel my life is slipping fast away—and you're not crying;
I look in devastation for your warmth—and you have gone!
Agony most cruel… left in solitude,
Forgotten ever after—you moved on!

CHORUS

I'd had enough, and in my rush to be done
Went like a fiend unfurled
Who wandered lost, nor could meet you once
Down the streets of the world…
And I'm lost in the wilds, like a nestless bird,
Like a small abandoned child,
With my sorrows clutching after me like claws
And tearing out my heart!

VERSE 2

Alley in the dark… night that never ends…
Shadows… coldness!
Funny that you came here to forgive
And to be kind…
Now my wretched life is at an end, and I'm a hollow…
Dead to all the world, and to you, my empty heart!
Agony most cruel… left in solitude,
To whimper ever after—nothing more!

RONDANDO TU ESQUINA

ENRIQUE CADÍCAMO, 1945

VERSO 1

Esta noche tengo ganas de buscarla,
de borrar lo que ha pasado y perdonarla.
Ya no me importa el que diran
ni de las cosas que hablarán…
¡Total la gente siempre habla!
Yo no pienso más que en ella a toda hora…
Es terrible esta pasión devoradora.
Y ella siempre sin saber,
sin siquiera sospechar
mis deseos de volver…

ESTRIBILLO

¿Que me has dado, vida mia,
que ando triste noche y dia?
Rondando siempre tu esquina,
mirando siempre tu casa,
y esta pasión que lastima,
y este dolor que no pasa…
¿Hasta cuando iré sufriendo
el tormento de tu amor?

VERSO 2

Este pobre corazón que no la olvida
me la nombra con los labios de su herida
y ahondando más su sinsabor
la mariposa del dolor
cruza en la noche de mi vida.
Compañeros, hoy es noche de verbena…
Sin embargo, yo no puedo con mi pena,
y al saber que ya no está,
solo, triste y sin amor
me pregunto sin cesar.

HANGING ROUND YOUR CORNER

ENRIQUE CADÍCAMO, 1945

VERSE 1

Here tonight I have an urge to go and find her,
To clear it up, forgive, and put it all behind her.
It doesn't matter what they say,
Or how they talk and talk away…
They're always talking, people, aren't they!
All I think about is her at every hour…
What a devil is this passion that devours!
And she might never even learn,
Never guess as we're apart
All I want is to return…

CHORUS

Life of mine, what have you brought me,
That night and day now has so distraught me?
Hanging always round your corner,
Looking always at your house there,
And all this passion that's such torture,
And this despond that sticks around me…
How much longer must I suffer
In the torment of this love?

VERSE 2

This poor heart of mine that can't forget about her
By the wound she left keeps calling to her louder,
And sinking deeper into loss,
The moth of grieving flies across
The night my life has been without her.
Friends, tonight the revels last until tomorrow…
But, for me, I can no longer take my sorrow,
And at the thought that she is gone,
Sadly, lovelessly, alone,
I keep asking on and on…

TU ÍNTIMO SECRETO

HÉCTOR MARCÓ, 1945

VERSO 1

La dicha es un castillo con un puente de cristal,
camina suavemente si lo quieres alcanzar.
Acércame tus labios sin odio, sin rencor,
desecha tus temores y entrégate al amor.
Tu íntimo secreto a nadie le confíes,
que el mundo siempre ríe y es muy calumniador.
La dicha es un castillo con un puente de cristal,
de mil que lo cruzamos, dos o tres suelen llegar.

ESTRIBILLO

Ven, mira que hermosa está la luna,
ven, reclínate en mi corazón…
Ríe, que nuestro enojo pasará
y un beso colmará
mi desesperación.
Ven, se que tus ojos están tristes,
hay remordimientos en tu voz,
y si me dejas morir
comenzarás a sufrir
cuando la seda de tu pañuelo
me diga adiós.

VERSO 2

La dicha es un castillo con un puente de cristal,
camina suavemente si lo quieres alcanzar.
Un alma incomparable te di para querer,
un alma, ¡oh!, que tu alma no sabe comprender,
y en un cielo de olvido, lo harás por esta pena,
quemar, como se quema un globo de papel.
La dicha es un castillo con un puente de cristal,
por él va mi cariño, acompáñalo a llegar.

YOUR INNERMOST OF SECRETS

HÉCTOR MARCÓ, 1945

VERSE 1

True bliss is like a castle with a bridge made out of glass,
Go walking ever softly if you wish to safely pass.
Just bring your lips in closer, no hatred, and no grudge;
Just cast away your worries and give yourself to love.
Your innermost of secrets confess to no one's ear,
For the world always sneers and is slanderous to judge.
True bliss is like a castle with bridge made out of glass,
Of thousands who go crossing, two or three arrive at last.

CHORUS

Come, and see how pretty the moon is…
Come, and lay your head on my heart…
Laugh now, for our chagrin shall pass away,
And a kiss will soon allay
The despair on my part.
Come, I know your eyes are full of sadness…
There, there's some misgiving in your voice…
And if you leave me to die,
You'll surely suffer and cry
When by the silk of your shawl you bid me
A last goodbye.

VERSE 2

True bliss is like a castle with a bridge made out of glass,
Go walking down it softly if you wish to safely pass.
A soul beyond compare I placed within your hands,
A soul, alas, your own soul could never understand,
And in the sky's oblivion you'll set it for its pains
On fire, in a ball of flame just like a paper lamp.
True bliss is like a castle with a bridge made out of glass,
My sweetheart goes across it, help her make her way at last.

THE AUTHORS

LUIS CÉSAR AMADORI (1902-1977) was an Italian-born film director and screenwriter in Argentina, who began his creative work writing for the stage after starting out in journalism. During his busy career, in which he sometimes used the pen name Leo Carter, he directed 78 films and wrote more than 50. His 1948 hit *Dios se lo pague* (May God Repay You) was selected for inclusion in the Oscars of that year. In the 1930s, Amadori collaborated on several tangos with Francisco Canaro, most notably "Madreselva," and cowrote some lyrics with E. S. Discépolo for the 1935 film *El Alma Del Bandoneón*, directed by Amadori's first directing partner Mario Soffici. When the Perón government was overthrown in 1955, Amadori moved to Spain, where in exile he directed two more films before finally returning to Buenos Aires in 1970.

ENRIQUE CADÍCAMO (1900-1999) wrote dozens of tango lyrics that anchor the songbook of the 1930s and 40s. A frequent collaborator of Juan Carlos Cobián, one of the tango's early tunesmiths, Cadícamo not only penned new hits but added fresh lyrics to old instrumentals, achieving a singular success in this approach with classics such as "Los mareados" (a song repurposed from an earlier play) and "Shusheta," written decades earlier without words. Alternately making memorable characters ("Muñeca brava," "Madame Ivonne"), capturing the city's moody scenery ("Nieblas del Riachuelo"), and painting memorable portraits of inward emotion ("Nostalgias"), Cadícamo's many lyrics of the highest quality help establish the center of the tango genre.

MIGUEL CALÓ (1907-1972) was a bandoneonist and bandleader whose *Orquesta de las estrellas* brought a sleek new sound to the tangos of the 1940s, maintaining its dance tempo while smoothing out the beat into a classy and lyrical style. Alongside his pianist Osmar Maderna, Caló co-authored both the lyrics and music for two of the group's hit songs, "Qué te importa que te llore" and "Jamás retornarás." After the wildly successful group split up into several separate orchestras—including those led by bandoneonist Domingo Federico; bandoneonist Julián Plaza (who worked with Troilo as well); the joint venture between bandoneonist Armando Pontier and violinist Enrique Francini; violinist Antonio Rodio; and double bassist Ariel Pedernera. Caló continued leading a band under his own name for decades, and in the early 1960s he and his former sidemen reconvened the "all-stars" orchestra to perform and record with the group's emblematic early singers Raúl Berón and Alberto Podestá.

CÁTULO CASTILLO (1906-1975) was the son of playwright and lyricist José González Castillo ("Griseta," "Sobre el pucho"), and began his career composing music for his father's verses. Together the two coauthored several classics of the genre, such as "Organito de la tarde" (1924) and "El aguacero" (1931). Cátulo later turned his hand to lyrics, bringing his father's sensitive lyricism to greater depths with dozens of tangos that came to redefine the songbook, such as "Tinta roja" (1941), "María" (1945), and "La última curda" (1956), these latter two with music composed by his close friend and frequent collaborator Aníbal Troilo. As the Golden Age of the tango drew to a close during the 1950s, the younger Castillo, with his potent blending of nostalgia and symbolism, proved to be the last great lyricist in the genre, and continued exploring new paths in songwriting through "Desencuentro" (1962) and the retrospective "Tiempo de percal" (1970).

JOSÉ MARÍA CONTURSI (1911-1972) was born in Buenos Aires, the son of lyricist Pascual Contursi. While working as a radio announcer in the early 1930s, Katunga, as his friends called him, chanced to meet the young Susana Gricel Viganó, who was visiting the city from her family country home in Córdoba. Soon followed a brief affair in her hometown, after which the two lived their separate lives; but she would prove to become his muse for the next twenty years, as he penned song after song over his feelings for her, bringing songs of romantic torment and frustrated longing to the forefront of the genre, eclipsing the social chronicle as the tango's central theme. As the Petrarch of the tango songbook, Contursi became the de facto leader of the new songwriting of the 1940s, with its focus on love and its eschewing of slang and character-based writing. His dozens of hits include "En esta tarde gris," "Cristal," "Garras," "Quiero verte una vez más," and, of course, "Gricel." Near the end of his life, when he was a widower and Gricel was estranged from her husband, the two reunited and eventually were able to marry, decades after believing the love of their youth was lost.

ENRIQUE SANTOS DISCÉPOLO (1901-1951) was born on March 27, 1901, into an artistic family. His father Enrique Santos was the Italian musican who taught music theory to the seminal early tango composer Ángel Villoldo; and his older brother Armando Discépolo was a playwright who created the genre known as *grosteco criollo*, a mix of the Italian grosteque and the *sainete criollo* or one-act farce, a precursor of today's sit-com. Becoming a stage actor by age sixteen, he pursued the entertainer's career of the time, becoming proficient in all facets of the performing arts. His earliest song of note was the outrageously sarcastic "Que vachaché" (1926), a street slang send-up of materialism, sharply critiquing a society whose only real value was expendable cash. The tune was booed at early performances, but the young Tita Merello brought it to prominence and it was recorded by Carlos Gardel in 1928. That same year saw his first bona-fide hit, the glaring satire "Esta noche me emborracho" (1928), which was soon followed by his anthemic protest tangos "Yira, yira" (1929) and "Cambalache" (1934). Later in his career, Discépolo wrote the harrowingly inward songs "Tormenta" (1939, used for a joke in his film *Cuatro corazones*), "Uno" (1943), and "Sin Palabras" (1946), before penning a new set of iconic lyrics for "El Choclo" (1947), the so-called national anthem of the tango. After a career encompassing screenwriting and directing, acting, composing film scores and songs, and even leading an orchestra, Discépolo fell ill after a heart attack and passed away on Dec. 23, 1951. His towering achievement as a songwriter comprises just 35 tunes—some of those being foxtrots and occasional numbers for stage and cinema.

HOMERO EXPÓSITO (1918-1987) shaped the tango of the 1940s with his lyrics of great evocative power and elliptical imagery, and his work is viewed by many as the culmination of the poetic movement in the genre. His songs, some of which feature his brother Virgilio's music, often develop an impressionistic landscape that echoes earlier songs, creating an aura of symbolism around tango details such as the balcony of the young girl ("Pedacito de cielo," 1942); the bustling city of Buenos Aires ("Tristezas de la calle Corrientes," 1942); the old gas streetlight ("Farol," 1943); the long skirt worn by girls in the old suburbs ("Percal," 1943); and the alley, the gate, and the grass ("Yuyo verde," 1944). His most famous song is perhaps the one with the most original imagery for a tango, "Naranjo en flor" (1944), likening a young girl to an orange tree in bloom.

CELEDONIO ESTEBAN FLORES (1896-1947) became the tango's foremost *lunfardo* poet, and began his career penning verse for print. His first recognition came in 1919, when his lyric "Por la pinta" won a prestigious newspaper contest; it was later set to music by Gardel and Razzano and retitled "Margot." The most famous Flores lyric is perhaps "Mano a mano" (1923), whose abundant slang and picturesque scenes portray the demimonde of the roaring '20s, so prominent in early tango lyrics. Other songs of his offer the local flavor of barrio life ("El bulín de la calle Ayacucho," 1925) alongside the street ethics of the hood ("Muchacho," 1926) and a virtual memorial of the times ("Corrientes y Esmeralda," 1933).

FRANCISCO GARCÍA JIMÉNEZ (1899-1983) brought a new sophistication to tango lyrics in the 1920s, developing the genre with extended metaphors in tunes such as "Zorro gris" (1921) and "Suerte loca" (1924), soon followed by "Príncipe" (1924), "La mentirosa" (1924), "Alma en pena" (1928), and "Palomita blanca" (1929), which favored extended metaphors and seriocomic situations instead of *lunfardo* and the typical bohemian settings. His talent peaked early, yet later in his career he added to his catalogue such classics of the 1940s as "Oigo tu voz" (1943), "Malvón" (1944), and "Rosicler" (1946). Besides writing lyrics himself, García Jiménez chronicled the songwriters of the times, and his first-hand account of the era's creative figures in such books as *Así nacieron los tangos* offers the most reliable group portrait of the Golden Age in its formative moments.

ALFREDO LE PERA (1900-1935), was born in São Paulo, Brazil, and lived in Buenos Aires from the time he was two months old. Like many budding lyricists he first entered the field of journalism, and while writing for *El Mundo* in 1928 he traveled as a foreign correspondent to the United States and Europe. Upon his return, he began writing subtitles for the United Artists movie studio, and his first song "Carillón de la Merced," co-authored with E. S. Discépolo, appeared in 1931. While staying in Paris in 1932, Le Pera crossed paths at the Paramount movie studio with Carlos Gardel, whom he had met before during his previous travels in Europe; and from that time onward, he became Gardel's chief songwriting partner and the screenwriter for his movies. Their films together include *Espérame* (1933), *La casa es seria* (1933), *Melodía de arrabal* (1933), *Cuesto abajo* (1934), *El tango de Broadway* (1935), *El día que me quieras* (1935, released 1936), and *Tango bar* (1935). Le Pera's style is noted for its "clean" and universal Spanish, which strove to resonate with an international audience, an ambition no doubt influenced by his work on subtitles as much as by any desire for commercial success. Gardel and Le Pera both died in a tragic plane accident in Medellín, Colombia, on June 24, 1935.

SAMUEL LINNIG (1888-1925) was born in Montevideo, Uruguay, and worked in Buenos Aires as a playwright, journalist, and photographer. The two hit songs of his career were both set-pieces in short plays (*sainetes*) that were otherwise absolute failures: "Milonguita" in the one-act *Delikatessen Haus* (co-written with Alberto Weisbach); and the tango "Melenita de oro" in his follow-up play *Milonguita*, which audiences voted the worst play of the year. Linnig, who also spelled his name Linning (like his father), was known to be a smart dresser who always appeared with white gloves and a cane, and he was also an inveterate gambler. He died of a sudden fever from unknown causes in 1925.

OSMAR MADERNA (1918-1951) was a pianist whose subtlety and romantic style earned him recognitin as "the Chopin of the tango." As the center of the *Orquesta de las estrellas* led by Miguel Caló, Maderna brought a sleek and chic sound to the tangos of the 1940s, smoothing the punchy rhythmic style then popular into a classy and eminently danceable glide. After cutting more than 80 recordings—including "Qué te importa que te llore" and "Jamás retornarás," both with lyrics and music co-authored by Maderna and Caló—the pianist branched out to form his own group in 1945, and recorded dozens of further tunes developing a clearer and refined style. He died during a crash while piloting his own small plane in 1951.

HOMERO MANZI (Homero Manzione, 1907-1951) was among the greatest and most influential of tango lyricists, raising the poetic quality of the genre such that others found a certain leadership in his work and were inspired to emulate his ambitious aesthetic vision. He also drew heavily on previous tangos, creating a strong network of imagery within the genre and a continuity between old styles and new directions. Manzi co-created the new *milonga* genre in the 1930s with composer Sebastian Piana; and his 1940s masterpieces "Malena," "Fuimos," and "Sur" (among many other classic songs) brought a new vision to the tango's established characters and conventions. In addition to writing lyrics, Manzi was also a magazine founder and trade union leader, and he wrote and directed movies as well; his rewrite of the old waltz "Desde el alma" for his 1948 film *Pobre mi madre querida* made that tune an all-time classic. After writing the tribute tango "Discepolín" to his friend, Manzi succumbed to cancer at age 43; and with Discépolo's own death at the end of that same year, the tango lost two of its leading creative talents.

HÉCTOR MARCÓ (Hector Marcolongo, 1906-1987) developed his songwriting talents in the 1920s and '30s while working as a singer and radio actor (appearing in Alberto Vaccarezza's radio soap opera *Sainetes porteños* among others), with some forays onto the stage. His early success with the waltz "Alma mía" gained him the favor of bandleader Carlos Di Sarli; and after co-writing the tango "Corazón" (at a bar, Di Sarli hummed the melody and Marcó told him the title), the two embarked upon a fruitful collaboration which produced dozens of songs. Marcó's lyrics bear some similarity to opera arias, and are noted for their directness and sentimentality; his use of bridges and stanzas of uneven lengths pushed the tango into freer formal territory, an expressive pursuit and achievement he shared with the great romantic lyricist José María Contursi.

MARVIL (Elizardo Martínez Vilas, 1902-1976) was a lyricist active from the 1930s through the 1950s, whose work was admired for its polish and its occasional delving into comic territory. Along with Elías Randal working as composer, he cowrote the songs "Así se canta" (1943), "Mi tango es triste" (1944), and the milonga "Oiga rubia" (1944). His other hits among a few dozen numbers include "Y sonó el despertador" (1944), "Buzón" and "Anselmo Laguna" (1945), "La vida me engañó" and "Se lustra, señor?" (1946), "Cómo nos cambia la vida" (1952), and "En tus brazos" (1958)—the last of these the basis of the award-winning animation short *En tus brazos* (2006).

GABINO CORIA PEÑALOZA (1881-1975) was a poet and lyricist, whose first forays into tango found him working alongside composer Juan de Dios Filiberto and singer Carlos Gardel. His earliest tango was "El pañuelito" (1920), and "Caminito" (1926) is by far his most renowned work in the genre. The story that it refers to an old footpath in the La Boca neighborhood is apocryphal, and a tale he never endorsed, although his friend, the painter Benito Quinquela Martín, used it as a pretext in the 1950s for restoring the neighborhood, which currently features an open-air museum and tourist attraction named for the song. The actual origin of the song was a love affair Peñaloza had during his youth in the early 1900s: traveling by horse or mule through the remote La Rioja province while working as a vineyard inspector, he was waylaid by floods near the city of Olta, where he had a clandestine affair with a local girl. When he later returned to Olta, he found that the girl had fled after learning she was pregnant, and he remained unable to find her. Peñaloza later relocated to La Rioja and spent the remainder of his life there.

REINALDO PIGNATARO (n.d.-1947) left behind him few details about his life. He has three tango lyrics to his credit: "Tres chupetes" (1928) and "Che, bacana" (1929), both with music by pianist Guillermo Cavazza; and the more justly famous "No me pregunten por qué" (1935), with music by Carlos Di Sarli, who recorded it during the 1950s on three separate occasions.

MANUEL ROMERO (1891-1954) was a prolific playwright, screenwriter, film director, and lyricist, whose credits include more than 180 works for the stage and 53 movies, with dozens of tangos scattered among them. An extremely swift worker, he was known for cranking out productions with great popular appeal. His most cherished songs include "Patotero sentimental" (1922, from the one-act *El bailarín del cabaret*); "Buenos Aires" (1923, from the one-act *En el fango de Paris*); "Tiempos viejos" (1926, from the one-act *Los muchachos de antes no usaban gomina*, remade as a film in 1937); "Tomo y obligo" (1931, from the hit film *Las luces de Buenos Aires*, Gardel's first feature as an actor); "Noches de Buenos Aires" (1935, from the film of the same name); and "Dime, mi amor" and "El vino triste" (1941, from the comic film *Yo quiero ser bataclana*).

OSCAR RUBENS (Oscar Rubistein, 1914-1984) was a lyricist and composer, and the second eldest of the four Rubistein brothers who worked in related parts of the tango world under a variety of pen-names. His brothers included songwriter and impresario Luis Rubistein (1908-1954), who founded a school for popular arts in the 1930s to train new talents for radio broadcasting; journalist and radio personality Mauri (Mauricio) Rubistein (1916-1984); and lyricist Elías Randal (Elías Rubistein, 1920-2005). Oscar's other hits, to name just a few tangos and waltzes in high rotation among dancers, include "Cuatro compases," "Lejos de Buenos Aires," and "El vals soñador" (from 1942); "Canta, pajarito," "Dejame así," and the waltz "Se fue" (from 1943); and "Calla, bandoneón," "Lloran las campanas," and yet another waltz, "Jugando, jugando" (from 1944).

HORACIO SANGUINETTI (Horacio Basterra, 1914-1957) wrote lyrics that were widely recorded by the top orchestras during the 1940s. Little is known of his personal life, aside from his birth in Montevideo (where he was also ultimately laid to rest) and his great success as a lyricist. Besides the ubiquitous topic of love, his recurring themes included the sea ("Tristeza marina"), Paris ("Ivon"), the Orient ("Gitana rusa"), and the African tambor or drum ("Alhucema"). In recent years a story has emerged that in 1950, at the funeral of his sister, who had died from tuberculosis, he confronted her widower (a military man) for having abused her, and on being threatened with a gun, shot the man himself. After fleeing to the house of his friend Osvaldo Pugliese, and later to the Chantecler club where he found Juan D'Arienzo,

Cátulo Castillo, and Homero Manzi, he was able to obtain an audience with Perón the following morning, who allowed him to sidestep prosecution for the murder and flee to Uruguay. The story is related by Oscar Del Priore and Irene Amuchástegui, and was corroborated by Beba Pugliese, the bandleader's daughter, in an interview with José María Otero in 2012.

NOTES

Tango belongs to a vast popular culture, spanning more than a century. Much of the secondary literature—interviews, articles, essays, memoirs, liner notes—is seldom well corroborated. Documentation often consists of anecdotes, audio recordings, sheet music printed during an era of censorship: not the most reliable of sources. Claims about the real-life identity of certain figures, such as "Malena," are notoriously suspect. Additionally, some of the influential histories of tango, such as the 1936 book *La historia del tango* by Héctor and Luis Bates, are riddled with errors and ulterior motives verging on propaganda; and more recent books, especially those by tourist authors, even unwittingly perpetuate certain falsehoods, offered by locals to amuse themselves at the expense of the gullible. The following notes therefore offer a mix of textual criticism, general research, and some interpretive conjecture.

Trustworthy scholarly studies about the early history of tango and of life in Buenos Aires, such as *Tango en la sociedad porteña: 1880-1920* by Hugo Lamas and Enrique Binda, have not yet changed the public imagination about tango and its origins, and a widespread conflation between subject and source remains prevalent. The fictions acted out in the songs are often mistaken for the songs' real origins. In short: the tango was probably never danced in brothels; it was abundantly popular among urban classes, both high and low, from the early 1900s onwards; photographs show it being danced in the tenements of the city's outskirts and also at the centennial presidential ball in 1905. Only the cattle-baron oligarchy, branding it immigrant music, denigrated the tango, and campaigned for country music to become the national culture instead. And for all that, the history of tango preceding the explosion of Tangomania in the 1910s, a story so often romanticized, has little bearing on what the tango became in the 1920s, once lyrics entered the picture.

With Pascual Contursi's rebranding of the instrumental tune "Lita" as "Mi noche triste," the genre moved from the parlor to the theater, as an offshoot of opera, making the tango, in effect, a character's aria on stage, in the middle of a one-act play. The outbreak of the Spanish influenza in 1918 delayed the development of the tango songbook by a few years; but with Samuel Linnig's "Milonguita" in 1920, the tango we know today stepped into the spotlight.

The booming industry of song, from its center in Buenos Aires, employed musicians and arrangers, composers and lyricists, producers, directors, scriptwriters, broadcasters, and singers. Sheet music and record sales formed the early commercial articles; stage shows were in high demand, and gradually became a movie industry, which by 1930 included sound films and spawned the hugely popular subgenre of tango films. Some of my notes below try to document these commercial origins of the music, following the changing face of show business as it evolved into new media.

Milonguita (1920)

LYRICS: Samuel Linnig
MUSIC: Enrique Delfino
From the one-act *Delikatessen Haus*
(S. Linnig & A. Weisbach)

TANGO LYRICS COLLECTIVELY comprise a kind of epic soap opera, and that poem's opening chapter centers on "Milonguita," the first tango of influence which was deliberately composed as a song with words from the outset.

Penned by debonair playwright (and inveterate gambler) Samuel Linnig, the song portrays a young woman of the suburbs, seduced by the tango to enter a life of luxurious debauchery working in the city nightclubs. Premiered by actress María Esther Podestá (to whom it was later dedicated), the song wound up being the single positive moment in the one-act farce *Delikatessen Haus*, which Linnig had co-written with Alberto Weisbach, and which proved to be such an unmitigated failure on the stage that Linnig, after parting the curtain to archly insult the play's hissing audience, had to sneak out the back of the playhouse in disguise.

"Milonguita" was not a runaway success immediately, and like many songs its fortune came as the result of several hands. Originally titled "Estercita" when delivered onstage by the character Blanca, director of a woman's orchestra, it caught the notice of Spanish theatrical singer Raquel Meller (1888-1962), one of the era's most famous entertainers (she appeared on the cover of *Time* in 1926). Meller added it to her act as a regular number, introducing the song to a much wider audience. Capitalizing on the newfound attention, Linnig soon wrote another one-act called *Milonguita*, featuring his only other song of note, "Melenita de oro" (Tresses of Gold).

Prior to this tango's immense popularity, the word *milonguita* evoked a simple coquette, a flapper working the nightclubs as a hired dancer as she sought a wealthy benefactor. In the wake of the song's fame, the word became forever linked to its tragic picture of urban nightlife and empty modern glamour, baptizing the tango as a new genre of storytelling song, a modern opera in miniature.

It is also important to recognize that this song, like some other early tangos, is not exactly pejorative in its portrayal of women. The original singer was the actress, speaking of her own character in the third person. While it is tempting to call Milonguita and the other *femmes* of tango lyrics "muses," they were not that at all: they were the subjects, the protagonists, much as they were in the popular demimonde operas of the day such as *Manon* and *La Bohème*.

VERSE 1

más linda 'e—i.e., *más linda de*.

la pollera cortona—This could also be interpreted to mean "your short skirts," as it was then the custom of country girls to wear skirts that ended above the ground; but "bashful skirts" is the more likely meaning in context, compared to the silk and furs of the nightclub. In any case, a *pollera* is a large long skirt, normally reaching below the ankle.

mujer—This appellation shows a touch of sympathetic insight: the girl (*pebeta*) is dreaming of her grown-up future as a woman (*mujer*).

algun tango—Already at its inception as a genre, one of the tango's major images is the tango itself.

CHORUS

Estercita—A name most likely chosen in homage to the actress María Esther Podestá (1896-1983), who premiered the song on stage. Linnig apparently titled the song "Estercita," until it became known under its usual title.

percal—Percale, a fine weave of cotton fabric, was once the chief textile from which women's skirts and house dresses were made, and thus evokes the life of decency and domesticity which this song's protagonist has left behind. More specifically, it refers to the long skirt or *pollera* mentioned in the first verse. The fabric became a recurring symbol in tangos—as evidenced in the colloquial phrase *cambiar el percal por la seda* (to trade percale for silk), and vice versa. Homero Expósito would later seize on this same symbol for his 1943 tango "Percal," which offers an impressionistic retelling of "Milonguita." Federico Silva also wrote a sequel song around 1968, titled "Otra vez Esthercita," which quips that now she wears "stretch" instead of percale.

Linnig himself may have lifted the image of percale from the opening verse of the Celedonio Flores poem "Por la pinta," which had won a big newspaper contest in 1919, and which later became the tango "Margot" when Gardel and Razzano set it to music in 1921. Both Linnig and Flores might also have been echoing the song "Con una falda de percal planchá" (With an Ironed Skirt of Percale), a well known *chotis* (schottische) from the 1896 zarzuela *Cuadros disolventes* (Solvent Paintings), with music by Manuel Nieto and words by Guillermo Perrín and Miguel de Palacios. This song was in circulation among Spanish singers well into the 1960s, with notable versions by star actresses Sarita Montiel and Olga Ramos.

VERSE 2

Cuando sales por la madrugada—The time here is just before sunrise (my usual translation of *madrugada* is "the dark of the morning"). This entire stanza, as I understand it, presents scenes of the girl's life in disjunction, and should probably not be read as a sequential narrative.

dicen que es el champán—This is possibly an echo of the Strauss operetta *Die Fledermaus* (1874), whose own story concludes quite farcically by blaming everything on champagne. The work remains enormously popular, with its performance having become a New Year's Eve tradition in Vienna.

Mano a mano (1923)

LYRICS: Celedonio Flores
MUSIC: Carlos Gardel & José Razzano

CONSIDERED AN EARLY masterpiece among tango lyrics, the *lunfardo*-heavy "Mano a mano" is perhaps the most famous work of Celedonio Flores—and is a song with its own controversies too. By turns it has been considered a sympathetic portrayal of women, or else male chauvinism incarnate, a fate perhaps inescapable for a tango that, like many others of this era, depicts the flapper's life in the heyday of the 1920s. Known as the Jazz Age in English, the time was a worldwide phenomenon whose anxiety-riddled excesses and boozy materialism bubbled up between the Spanish influenza at the end of the Great War in 1918 and the Great Depression of the 1930s. The flapper and her heedless lifestyle became the symbol of the age, in a display of liberated youth, neurotic hedonism, and clandestine debauchery.

Some sources claim that Flores wrote his text as early as 1920, the same year as "Milonguita"; a few others place it even earlier; but the song was not recorded until Gardel's first version in 1923. In any case, the lyrics were written first; and their poetic form (which Flores may have taken from Baudelaire,

Swinburne, or any number of late Nineteenth Century poets) posed Gardel and Razzano some difficulty, as they sought an appropriate musical setting. (They had already tackled the same form with the Flores poem "Por la pinta," retitled "Margot," in 1921.)

As usual, my translation follows the tune and rhythm of the original, and also draws on 1920s jive to convey the flavor and meaning of the *lunfardo* and to better represent the song's subject matter. Additionally, I emphasize some of the oddball choices in the original (such as *consecuente*, "accountable," in the first stanza, and *consejo*, advice or "information," in the last), which I read as Flores slyly tipping his hand, and showing that his portraiture is ironic and not quite to be taken at face value. As for the song's form: while all six stanzas use a single rhyme scheme (ABAAB), the melody uses an alternating verse-chorus structure, which I have marked accordingly.

VERSE 1

Rechiflao—This word, a favorite of Flores, connotes exasperation as well as infatuation, and was a common expression of the time. "Going crackers" is the period slang in English (meaning the same as "going nuts").

bacana—This word appears several times in this tango, meaning a flapper, a "made girl," and (in masculine form) a bigshot, which is its most usual sense in tangos. The word's exclamatory use (similar to "awesome" or "cool") comes from a later era. *Bacán* itself is a Genoese dialect word, denoting a wealthy man.

consecuente—An odd term (accountable) for a girlfriend, unless one is hiring her out.

CHORUS 1

el juego de remanye—A phrase whose meaning is now somewhat obscure. *Remanyar* derives from the Italian *mangiare*, "to eat," as a *vesre* (*revés* or back slang), but its meaning was "to recognize" and usually implied seeing through someone's pretenses to a real motive. Thus "the guessing game" in my translation.

Gambeteabas—A soccer term used for dribbling, often used by Flores with the sense of "shifting" (i.e., evading, improvising) or "making do."

morlaccos—Moolah.

a la marchanta—A now obscure phrase which essentially means "with abandon," like someone flinging things around carelessly.

VERSE 2

el mate—Lit., "your gourd" (also the cup for *yerba mate*).

te engrupieron—*Engrupir* can mean both "to lead on" and "to be puffed up," i.e., it can indicate either the deceit performed on someone, or the conceit entertained by oneself.

la milonga, entre magnates—Clearly, the *milonga* imagined in this song is a premiere upscale nightclub, and not the tenement parties of the slums.

CHORUS 2

Nada debo agradecerte—This statement is often interpreted to portray the speaker as an ingrate, withholding his thanks; but as the context of the stanza makes clear, he is more probably regretting that he owes her nothing because he no longer enjoys her favors or her company. My translation strives to work with either scenario.

en la cuenta del otario—This quip draws on a famous opera prank. Act 2 of *La Bohème* ends with the courtesan-singer Musetta charging her friends' restaurant bill to the rich admirer she is duping.

VERSE 3

que te abrás de las paradas—There are several variants of this somewhat difficult line, including *que te abrás en las paradas*, *que te habrás en las paradas* and *que te abracen las paradas*. The general sense of them all is "may you make a big splash at the hot spots."

CHORUS 3

mueble viejo—Lit., "old furniture." Given the habits of the elite at the time, this is perhaps best understood as meaning townhouse *décor*, last season's furnishings.

un consejo—Lit., "advice"; but the implication is more like "a tip" or "a lead," suggesting he could help find her next job. (I favor this reading especially because of the entire phrase's construction: "if you're short on advice.")

Caminito (1926)

LYRICS: Gabino Coria Peñaloza
MUSIC: Juan de Dios Filiberto

CAMINITO IS A real footpath in the southside of Buenos Aires which has seen a lot of changes, most of them unfortunate. Originally a rivulet of the Riachuelo river in La Boca (the neighborhood at the mouth of the river), it later dried up and was the site of some railroad tracks—carving out a "little footpath" which has been associated with this famous tango of 1926. Later, when the railway fell into disuse, the area became a landfill. During the 1950s, Argentina's foremost painter Benito Quinquela Martín, who lived nearby and was a friend of the tune's composer, began a project to rehabilitate the site; and in 1959, the mayor renamed a small lane "Caminito," to honor the tango.

This Caminito is today an outdoor museum and colorful tourist attraction.

Peñaloza, however, did not consent to the renaming. Despite the local lore surrounding the place, he insisted that the "caminito" of his lyrics belonged to a different place entirely. The poet's son Álvaro later recounted the story of his father's song, explaining that it refers to a love affair the poet had during the early 1900s, in the western La Rioja province of Argentina. The young Peñaloza, then traveling by mule or horse as a vineyard inspector, was waylaid by a flooded river that blocked his way near the town of Olta. While delayed there for several days, he met and pursued a clandestine affair with a local girl who was able to play the town's piano, then a rare item for that remote location. When he later returned to Olta for the girl, he found that she had fled the town, pregnant; and despite his efforts to locate her, they remained unable to reunite, nor ever had contact again.

It must be said that the lyrics match this story rather perfectly; and in light of this origin, the song's association with the footpath of La Boca seems rather forced. Yet this would not be the first time that an apocryphal story became a major part of tango history; and the story of the tango, as told both during and after the Golden Age, is quite literally riddled with mistruths.

On a sidenote: the lyrics of "Caminito" use assonance rhyme throughout (*pasar - mal*; *flor - yo*), which is acceptable in classic Spanish prosody; it is also quite common in songs, where vowels are of overriding importance.

VERSE 1

que el tiempo ha borrado—As noted above, the "Caminito" in Buenos Aires was formerly a riverbed, before it became a footpath beside some railroad tracks, overgrown with plants. These circumstances make it tempting to associate the song with that location.

CHORUS

Desde que se fue—While the theme of the gone beloved is common to many genres of song, it fits especially well with the early tango's lament over girls leaving the country and the outskirts to plunge into urban debauchery in the cities. That is not what this song is about (see introductory note above); yet it harmonizes with the themes of many other tangos from the 1920s.

VERSE 2

que mi llanto tu suelo regó—This image of tears wetting the ground would elliptically relate to the Buenos Aires footpath's past as a rivulet. However, it more directly relates to the flooded river which delayed Peñaloza in Olta. (The tears, in either case, figuratively recapitulate the past of the trail.)

Alma en pena (1928)

LYRICS: Francisco García Jiménez
MUSIC: Anselmo Aieta
Basis of the film *Alma en pena*
(Dir. Julio Irigoyen, 1928)

THE DEGREE OF wit with which García Jiménez invested this finely crafted song, among several others he had penned in the 1920s, constitutes his permanent contribution to the genre. His urbane lyricism served to raise the tango's style and subject matter above the grit and grime of its origins; he brought a suave irony into play, counterbalancing the streetwise cleverness of early lunfardo-laden songs such as those of Pascual Contursi and Celedonio Flores. Like other great tangos of the era, this song portrays a character in a theatrical situation, its few verses evoking what seems to be a larger, more extended story in the background.

This song also lent its title to the 1928 silent film *Alma en pena*, directed by Julio Irigoyen, which itself launched the subgenre of the "tango movie." Within two years, the first sound films were appearing in Argentina, and their popularity soon led them to rival (and eventually to eclipse) the theater as a venue for new songs.

The verses of "Alma en pena" use a witty rhythm that juggles the line segments back and forth, as though passing them from one hand to the other, in expression of an internal debate. Setting these lines on the page to show a proper four phrases would unfortunately conceal their intuitive flow, so instead I have arranged them to indicate the two halves of the stanza: please interpret each of these halves as containing two phrases apiece. (The chorus, meanwhile, works in a more familiar manner.)

VERSE 1

Aún el tiempo no logró—Because of how this song's melodic motif enters late (i.e., on *llevar* in the line below this one), the entire first line of the verse has the effect of occurring in a pickup measure. The half-lines that follow repeat a staccato figure which syncopates the stanza as a whole, making the "second" hemistichs seem like the "first," and vice versa. The effect is an ingenious representation of the speaker's anxiety. My arrangement on the page attempts to show this inverted structure without being too distracting.

CHORUS

Alma—The first two phrases of the chorus begin soberly on the downbeat, in contrast with the verses' offset rhythm mentioned above. The third and fourth phrases of the chorus slip back into anticipation, beginning a measure early (*Tú me ense|ñaste a querer…*)

mendrugos del olvido—This witty simile ("crusts of that forgetting") is almost worth the entire song. *Mendrugo* (crust) also means dimwit.

VERSE 2

limosna—Lit. "alms."

Madreselva (1931)

LYRICS: Luis César Amadori
MUSIC: Francisco Canaro
Featured in the play *Madreselva* (Amadori, 1931)
and the film *Madreselva* (dir. Amadori, 1938)

THANKS TO ITS central role in the 1938 film of the same name, the tango "Madreselva" has come to be known as a something of a cinematic set-piece, and perhaps also as a tear-jerker. With its combination of nostalgia and sentiment, the song proved an effective vehicle for the emotions at the center of its larger story.

The celebrated actress and singer Libertad Lamarque starred in the film, singing this tango early in the action, and then once again in the stirring final scene, before an audience at a large concert hall. While the lyrics are written for a female character, they may be sung by a male singer with no alterations necessary. In the year of the film's release, Francisco Canaro recorded the song with Roberto Maida singing, and Francisco Lomuto recorded it with Jorge Omar providing the vocals, at a slightly faster pace. Ángel Vargas recorded a version with Ángel D'Agostino's band in 1944. Since then the tune has become a classic of the repertoire, sometimes even performed in instrumental arrangements (by Miguel Villasboas among others).

VERSE 1

Vieja pared—Neighborhoods throughout Latin America (including south Florida in the United States) are often demarcated by boundary walls. The opening of "Tinta roja" refers to such a *paredon* as well, possibly echoing this song's opening amid its own flood of memories.

BRIDGE

Pasaron los años—This brief interlude or bridge is rarely seen in the tango during this era. It would later become a feature favored by certain authors, such as Héctor Marcó (e.g., in "Esta noche de luna" and "Nido gaucho").

VERSE 2

que amor y fe mentiras son—Possibly an echo of the sterner lines that begin the refrain of Discépolo's 1929 tango "Yira, yira": *Verás que todo es mentira, Verás que nada es amor* (You'll see it's all just a swindle, You'll see there ain't any love). Amadori and Discépolo were later to collaborate on the film *El Alma del Bandoneón* in 1935.

Cambalache (1934)

LYRICS & MUSIC: Enrique Santos Discépolo
Featured in the film *El alma del bandoneón*
(Dir. Mario Soffici, 1935)

DISCÉPOLO'S ANTHEMIC PROTEST song "Cambalache" is one of the few tangos that transcends the genre entirely, and it has been adapted by punk bands as well as crossover hip-hop artists. Written in 1934 amid Argentina's "Decade of Infamy" during the Great Depression, the song gave voice to the disaffected in the face of widespread corruption and lost opportunities for progress. It first appeared in the 1935 film *El Alma Del Bandoneón*, directed by Mario Soffici, which is considered an early classic of Argentine cinema. (Ernesto Famá, playing a singer in a radio studio, performs it in the movie while people around the country listen at their radio receivers.)

The song's title and central metaphor derive from the "hockshop" at the heart of the Stavisky affair, the false store where that embezzler conducted the fraudulent investment scheme that ensnared several of France's most prominent politicians, and whose exposure resulted in the downfall of the French government. The passage in the third stanza, which depicts many names of the day jumbled together, including Stavisky's, was feasibly taken straight from a real page of a 1934 newspaper, since some of the names have more than one topical reference. That the names have little to do with each other, and yet appear together as an emblem of the times, would indeed seem to be the entire point of the mashup. My notes below explore this in more detail.

The later image of the Bible—sadly affixed to a wire hook for use as toilet paper, as recently explained by an anonymous commentator online—was for many years considered somewhat obscure.

VERSE 1

quinientos seis—The year 1506 was formerly taught as the date when Portuguese explorer Martim Afonso de Sousa (Martín Alfonso de Souza) founded the São Vicente (San Vicente) colony in Brazil, the first European settlement in South America. This dating appears throughout history books of the 1800s, and as late as Ruy Díaz de Guzmán's *Argentina* published in 1900; nowadays, however, the accepted date is 1532 (de Sousa's correct date of birth being 1500). Other notable events of 1506 include the death of Columbus; the massacre of thousands of Jews in Lisbon carried out by locals in a fit of religious fervor; and the first use of the term "America" to refer to the New World continents—albeit this last item was probably not widely known at the time. My translation substitutes 1492 for the year here, somewhat simplifying the point. (Note: the number in the lyrics is literally 506; but it is common in both Spanish and Italian to refer to years with the "mil" omitted, e.g., *cinquecento* for the 1500s, "Milonga del novecientos" for "Milonga of the 1900s.")

manoseaos—Lit., "manhandled" or "groped," with its meaning of sexual violation.

CHORUS 1

colchonero—Lit. "mattress maker," the term *colchonero* was also a nickname of the Madrid football team (Club Atlético de Madrid) due to their red and white striped uniforms.

rey de bastos—While "king of clubs" likely refers to a gangster, it could also be an elliptical term for a polo player.

VERSE 2

Alexandre ***Stavisky*** (1888-1934)—French-Ukrainian financier and fraud, whose "hockshop" was a front for selling phony bonds. When government ministers were implicated in his crimes, he fled to a chalet and was found "suicided" by the police, provoking riots in Paris that brought down the government.

Saint Giovanni ***Bosco*** (1815-1888)—Italian priest and educator who founded the Salesian Preventive Method of teaching, which was widely adopted in Argentina; he was canonized in 1934.

Mignón—A character in opera and popular culture (derived from Goethe's novel *Wilhelm Meister's Apprenticeship*); the name and image became a byword for chic fashion as well as illicit affairs. Mignón was also a popular brand of German typewriter, discontinued in 1934.

Don Chicho (1892-1943)—Born Giovanni Galiffi, Don Chicho was a Sicilian mobster who styled himself "the Al Capone of Rosario"; he was deported from Argentina to Italy in 1934.

Napoleon Bonaparte (1769-1821)—Appears in the title of the 1934 novel *A Spy of Napoleon*, by that era's immensely popular author Emma Orczy.

Primo ***Carnera*** (1906-1967)—Italian heavyweight boxer, who was world champion in 1933-1934; he still holds the record for most wins by knock-out (with 72).

José de ***San Martín*** (1778-1850)—Argentine general, the national hero and *liberador* of South America. More topically, the name also indicates Dr. Ramón Grau San Martín, who served temporarily as president of Cuba during the Hundred Days Government in 1934, following on heels of the Sergeants' Revolt which had overthrown the corrupt regime the previous year.

cambalaches—The front for Stavisky's fraudulent financial crimes was known as his "hockshop."

sable sin remaches—A slang term (rivetless sabre) for a wire hook.

CHORUS 2

Siglo veinte, cambalache—These words were appropriated for the title of a television talkshow in Argentina (*Siglo XX Cambalache*, 1992-1995).

el que vive de los otros—In Julio Sosa's famous 1955 rendition of this song, he replaces this line with *el que vive de las minas* (one who sponges off the ladies)—a nod to early tangos' depiction of procurers who lived off the gains of their ladyfriends.

No me pregunten por qué (1935)

LYRICS: Reinaldo Pignataro
MUSIC: Carlos Di Sarli

THIS MEMORABLE TANGO is one of several composed by the great pianist and bandleader Carlos Di Sarli, who recorded it no fewer than three times in the 1950s (twice with Mario Pomar and once again with Jorge Durán). The song had previously been a hit under the baton of Francisco Canaro with the strong vocal delivery of Ernesto Famá, which brings out the lyrics' endearing mixture of self-mocking humor and booze-and-blues regret. Such tragicomedy was of course not new to the tango, but in this song it seems on the verge of transition, like a moth cracking out of its coccoon, from the critical edge of the 1930s to the more romantic tangos of the following decade.

The sheet music for this tango prints each verse as two stanzas (the first half is the same both times), and also does not label any of the stanzas. Very little is known today of lyricist Reinaldo Pignataro, who also penned the tangos "Tres chupetes" and "Che, bacana" (the latter recorded by the Di Sarli sextet in 1929, perhaps unfortunately as an instrumental number).

VERSE 1

café—The terms *café* and *cafetín* refer to taverns, as in the Discépolo tango "Cafetín de Buenos Aires." Such establishments were usually gathering places where men could socialize separately from women. Café, of course, can also mean cabaret.

colo—A *vesre* (back slang) for *loco.*

CHORUS

Hoy que vivo—The speaker here does not say why he is no longer with the woman he loves, blaming the estrangement neither on her nor on other causes (the city, a rival, God). The theme of lost love was gradually abstracting itself out of the social chronicle; and taking the historical perspective, we can see how this tango was a prelude for "Nostalgias," and the many songs of J. M. Contursi which were about to hit the scene.

El día que me quieras (1935)

LYRICS: Alfredo Le Pera
MUSIC: Carlos Gardel
Featured in the film *El día que me quieras*
(Dir. Eduardo Morera, 1935)

THE TANGO'S GREATEST figure is Carlos Gardel, whose charisma on stage and screen was outdone only by his golden voice. As an established star, Gardel was a driving force behind early Argentine cinema: one of the first sound films was a compilation of him singing fifteen different songs, after chatting with their respective authors, in *Así cantaba Carlos Gardel* (1930, dir. Eduardo Morera). Just ten of those filmed performances survive today, but luckily Gardel starred in several other movies before his untimely death in a plane crash in 1935. The most finely made of the lot is *El día que me quieras* (1935, dir. John Reinhardt). Lyricist Alfredo Le Pera wrote the script and the lyrics for the songs, while Terig Tucci and Gardel collaborated on the film's music.

The title number, while not technically a tango (it is a *canción*, a ballad) has become one of the all-time classics of Argentina's popular music. It is not much played for dancing, due to the scarcity of recordings by Golden Age dance orchestras. Edgardo Donato's orchestra arranged it with a tango beat for a 1935 recording with singer Juan Alessio—who would become more widely known after 1939 under the stage name Jorge Ortiz.

The song appears twice in the film, first when the protagonist sings to his beloved Margarita, who joins him in a duet near the end; and then in a reprise at the end of the film, long after her death, when he sings with their daughter Marga (Rosita Moreno playing both roles). My interpretation of the title, which uses the subjunctive *quieras*, leaves the verb tense unresolved in order to convey a sense of yearning.

VERSE 1

Acaricia mi ensueño—Gardel delivers this opening verse *recitativo*, much as the verse of many Tin Pan Alley standards was performed during the same era, a practice with a long tradition in opera and other musical theater. (By comparison, in the second verse he speaks plainly, rather than reciting.)

ella acquieta mi herida—The change of rhythm here (from a three-part line to a two-part line) offers a good example of how the lyrics can "modulate" or dilate to a slower delivery, without any change in the tempo of the music.

CHORUS 2

La noche que me quieras—This stanza forms a second chorus for the song. In the film arrangement, this section is later repeated, without the first chorus, to conclude the tune.

las estrellas celosas—In Le Pera's lyrics for the tango "Volver," also featured in *El día que me quieras*, the stars are described in an adversarial role:

> *Bajo el burlón mirar de las estrellas*
> *que con indiferencia, hoy me ven volver.*
> (Under the stars that stare down wryly
> And with indifference, watch me now come home.)

VERSE 2

El día—This second full verse is given a spoken delivery by Gardel, making a third mode of vocal performance (after his *recitativo* opening in the first verse, and his normal singing in the chorus).

Alma del bandoneón (1935)

LYRICS: E. S. Discépolo & L. C. Amadori
MUSIC: Enrique Santos Discépolo
Featured in the film *El alma del bandoneón*
(Dir. Mario Soffici, 1935)

NOTES

Many tangos speak not only of, but directly to, the bandoneón. This instrument had by the 1930s become the most emblematic figure on the tango bandstand. Before this touching tune, there is a 1928 tango by Pascual Contursi called "Bandoneón arrabalero," which likewise addresses the melancholy squeezebox—but only Discépolo, who was responsible for most of this lyric, would have compared its bellows to a caterpillar.

This song is the title number of the 1935 film *El alma del bandoneón*, and plays a key part in the plot. To understand the title, we just need to read the bandoneón as the symbol of the tango itself, because the film is about the tango—not just as a style of music, but as a modern phenomenon permeating city life, the radio, and even the temples of high culture. The story revolves around Fabián (Santiago Arrieta), a young man sent to the city by his rancher father, to pursue a career he quickly abandons in favor of becoming a composer—of tangos, to which his father objects. In the finale, the leading lady Elda (Libertad Lamarque), who has joined in his endeavors, in order to pursue her own success as a singer, walks onstage at the Teatro Colón, Argentina's premier opera house, where an orchestra of 100 bandoneóns is playing this song's theme. As she joins in, singing the lyric, she soon wins over the audience, which includes the composer's father.

The film's main conflict, which pits the city tango against the country-based cattle barons (the oligarchy of Argentina), who favored the music now known as *folclore*, encapsulates the actual history of how the tango evolved and became the cultural icon not just of Buenos Aires but of Argentina.

VERSE 1

Yo me burlé de vos—The speaker of this lyric embodies the views of one who initially disparaged the tango. In the context of the film, this is obviously meant to resonate with the fictional composer's father.

Recién comprendo bien—This line sounds the motif of recognition or conscience, the deep content which is common to many tangos.

sos un oruga—The film's plot is a coming-of-age story, so the image of the bellows as a caterpillar, wishing to become a butterfly, cutely allegorizes the hero's struggle against his father.

CHORUS

la vida oscura y sin perdon—This life "obscure and never spared" (or never forgiven), which the tango itself represents in this song, is what awaits the hero of the film unless (i.e., until) his father relents.

VERSE 2

al apretarte en mis brazos—The sense here is that the speaker would squeeze the bandoneón as one embracing it. Of course, that is one way to sound the instrument (which is more often played while opening the bellows).

Nostalgias (1936)

LYRICS: Enrique Cadícamo
MUSIC: Juan Carlos Cobián

THE TANGO SONGBOOK is full of songwriting duos, and among the most successful partnerships was that of Cobián and Cadícamo. Theirs was both a fruitful collaboration and an exercise in recycling: Cobián had composed a number of instrumental melodies in the 1920s, which Cadícamo later baptized with fresh lyrics, often resulting in songs that gained a completely new identity. The tango "Los mareados" (featured further below) offers an instance of great distance between inception and reinvention, spanning decades and several different shows; but the difference between a song's initial departure into the world and its later arrival at fame, in quite a different direction than first intended, was sometimes less than a year.

Among the most notable successes that came of this process is the tango "Nostalgias." According to García Jimenez in his book *Así nacieron los tangos*, the song was first intended for Cadícamo's revue *El cantor de Buenos Aires*, written to mark the death of Gardel; but the show's producer rejected the number due to its complexity, and another was substituted in its place. The play opened in 1935 at the Smart theater (later the Blanco Podestá), but closed after a couple weeks without much ado. Later on, in 1936, the rejected song was repurposed for a performance at the Charleston club, featuring singer Rodríguez Lesende with Cobián leading the orchestra, and there the song gained great favor with the audience, rocketing to stardom and quickly becoming a standard in the repertoire. Despite only a few recordings by dance orchestras, "Nostalgias" was included in many films (starting in 1937 with *Así es el tango*, directed by Eduardo Morera); and after dozens of recordings by popular singers, it has entered the highest ranks of the tango songbook.

VERSE 1

Quiero emborrachar—The lyrics throughout the verse follow the staccato sixteenth-note melody of the song, a style of melody which is especially characteristic of the early tango.

otras bocas—I.e., the "mouth" of the bottle.

CHORUS

su risa loca—Mad laughter is a theme Cadícamo would reprise in "Los mareados" (1942).

Hermano—This to addressed to the bandoneón (as in the second verse).

no puedo—The melody here very significantly breaks the word *puedo* (I can) into two syllables, holding the first with a long note. There is no indication of this in the original lyric, but it is represented in my rendition by an ellipsis in the phrase.

Quiero verte una vez más (1939)

LYRICS: José María Contursi
MUSIC: Mario Canaro

THE NEW TANGOS of the 1940s bring to the genre a searing, earnest profession of love, perhaps a natural outcome of the early tango's prominent use of first-person narration, where a stage character speaks directly. The leading proponent of this shift towards romantic intensity on the verbal side was José María Contursi, known to his friends as Katunga. His father Pascual Contursi had himself broken new ground as the tango's first lyricist of lasting influence in the late 1910s, with the romantically oriented "Mi noche triste"; and just as his father turned away from the parlor-music trivialities of the tango's origin, so too did this second-generation tango poet turn aside from the dominant style of the day, to pursue a new aesthetic immersed in the theme of love.

Love songs can seem thematically simple because they are so familiar, but Contursi's work as a lyricist draws more deeply on the traditions of European poetry than may be apparent at first glance. His constant, even obsessive harping on the dual themes of regret and desire, may well come from his personal experience; but his poetic tools come from Petrarch; and his restless exploration of form, which has been quite overlooked by tango commentators, shows his very conscious awareness of how emotional traction in song is the result of expert craftsmanship.

As an instance of this last element, one may observe that "Quiero verte una vez mas"—was there ever a more straightforward title?—uses a double-length chorus, a feature common in jazz standards but quite rare in tangos. Contursi was to use this structure again in his 1941 hit "En esta tarde gris." Arguably it was Contursi's formal innovation in the beginning of the decade that paved the way for poets like Héctor Marcó, just a year or two later, to follow in this direction (his "Esta noche de luna" likewise features a double-length chorus).

Aside from this formal aspect, this song does not yet show Contursi's fresh imagery; and what would later become his white-hot lyricism of yearning is just warming up here. Indeed this song appears almost deliberately generic, and was perhaps a trial run of the more personal, direct type of song, which the young poet was ready to make his signature.

CHORUS

pupilas—"Pupils" for "eyes" is a conspicuously literary usage, perhaps indicating Contursi's conscious effort to draw on traditional poetic models.

las cenizas de un amor—As an image of romantic aftermath, "the ashes of a love" links this song to Contursi's later lyrics, where he evokes and laments his love for Gricel in similar terms (broken glass, etc.)

por que te fuiste—Only at this point, more than halfway through the chorus, does the plot of the song emerge: she is the one who left. This detail, so extraneous to the rest of the text, seems like an afterthought, likely an indication that Contursi was imitating other songs. In particular, this case of the man abandoned by a woman comes from the early tango songbook, notably from "Mi noche triste," written by the poet's father Pascual Contursi.

VERSE 2

Noche—The four phrases of this second verse begin bluntly, each line launching from a poetic motif: *noche* (night), *quejas* (groans or sobs), *sangre* (blood), *fiebre* (fever). These images, common to both the tango and the Petrarchan idiom, make it seem almost like the young craftsman was going down a checklist as he filled in the words for this stanza.

Tinta roja (1941)

LYRICS: Cátulo Castillo
MUSIC: Sebastián Piana

ONE OF THE best examples in the repertoire of an impressionistic tango, which works by a kind of free association of images and loosely organized details, is this nostalgic "Tinta roja." This catchy song with its evocation of the old neighborhoods in Buenos Aires, a frequent theme in tangos, is now a classic of the genre. At its debut in 1941, however, it was not a big success, and it was not recorded widely during the Golden Age.

The song works almost entirely through images of the streets, connected intuitively. First, then, a word about the title. Red ink is primarily a floating, unattached metaphor in these lyrics: it stands for the brick of the barrio wall, the cheap wine of the tavern, the maroon postboxes imported from England, the red tunic of the patrolman, the hot blood of the speaker—it is, in short, an organizing motif for every detail in the verses, like a team color for the poet's memory. At the same time, red ink has two other associations which add to the atmosphere and meaning of the song. First and more familiar, is sepia toning, the reddish-brown tint (literally ink of the cuttlefish) which has been used to give images an "antique" look since the 1800s. The second connotation lies in everyday customs of a bygone era, and is possibly what Castillo had in mind all along: in former times, red ink was commonly available at pharmacies, because it was the color most people used when writing in their personal journals.

As for the form of the lyrics: Castillo's verse is often acrobatic and replete with rhyme, which leads many editions to break up his lines into very small segments on the page, as though they were a set of free-standing haikus. I resist that temptation here, preferring to show the melodic phrase more clearly, and to indicate at least an outline of the more familiar "block" stanza which was no doubt his model.

VERSE 1

Paredón—The boundary wall around the neighborhood, a feature common to many residential areas in the Latin world. Such a wall (*pared*) also appears prominently in "Madreselva."

tinta roja—Red ink was once widely used by many people for writing in their journals, and was widely available in pharmacies. Red ink also suggests sepia toning, used for antique images since the early 1800s, and similar to other methods used for centuries.

botón—Like "buttons" in English, which was slang in the jazz age, this is a metonymic term denoting a policeman by the uniform's brass buttons. Castillo may have chosen this figure because of the white-belted maroon tunics, with their single row of closely spaced buttons, which were worn by patrolmen in Buenos Aires at certain periods, but I have not been able to verify that these were the uniforms used in the era most likely evoked in this song (the 1910s).

buzón carmin—Red pillarboxes, imported into Buenos Aires from England, were a common feature in the city during the early 1900s, and some still function today as postal drops.

tano—An Italian; contraction of *italiano* ("paisan" is my preference in English, to capture the sense of an immigrant, while avoiding slurs).

bon vin—A common euphemism for the cheap house wine sold in saloons; it is mock French, pronounced as Spanish.

CHORUS

raso—*Raso* also means "satin"; but its primary meaning (and its obvious sense in this song) is "cloudless."

pedazo—*Pedazo* (piece) is a common word in tango lyrics, indicating a general diminutive ("a bit") as well as fragmentation. Its use here in a song evoking the old neighborhood of the poet's youth perhaps inspired Homero Manzi's great tango on the same theme, "Barrio de Tango" of 1942, which opens with the words *Un pedazo de barrio* (A small piece of a barrio). Manzi's tango also echoes the hiding (*escondía*) of the poet's love—here behind a window (*balcón*), and in Manzi's lyric behind a gate (*portón*).

Qué te importa que te llore (1942)

LYRICS & MUSIC: Osmar Maderna & Miguel Caló

ONE OF THE tango bands that best represented the sleek new sound of the '40s was Miguel Caló's *Orquesta de las Estrellas* (All-Star Orchestra). The group deserved the name not just because it was packed with talented young sidemen, but also because many of them were songwriters too, and in various combinations were literally penning the tango's new songbook. When the group began splitting up around 1945, the pianist Osmar Maderna, whose presence had brought the ensemble its sparkle and classy ambience, was widely considered the brightest talent of the bunch. His promising career ended early after a fatal car accident in 1951.

There is little historical importance to the tango "Qué te importa que te llore": it is here purely because so many dancers adore its rhythm and vibe. The authorship of both the tune and the words is credited jointly to Caló and Maderna (who also cowrote the tango "Jamás retornarás"), so we cannot say who wrote what precisely; but the lyrics do bear some interesting features. The verbal backtracking and repetition in the opening lines is an original device, which both builds up the song's rhythm and conveys the speaker's obsessive and uncertain mood. The use of metaphor in the refrain is also a bit unusual for a tango: it is more typical of the genre to show situations, but here the developed analogical imagery seems more reminiscent of a written poem.

VERSE 1

Déjame mentir—To paraphrase: the speaker knows that he is lying to himself, that he wishes for his beloved in vain, yet he wants to be left with his wish because—he now understands—it is also his memory (*esperar es un pedazo de recuerdo,* yearning is a bit of recollection). Such procedures continue throughout the song, as each new theme unravels under the speaker's self-examination. This psychological realism in the portrayal of sentiment, which explores how yearning leads to self-deception, and how the conscious awareness of this interferes with both, shows the casual influence of Freud in Argentina.

que volverás—The backtracking repetition of these words employs a novel verbal device, which represents the speaker fretting and reversing over his thoughts, somewhat neurotically. (Technically, this might be called medial anaphora.) The melody here matches this perfectly, running up and down the same arpeggio twice, until it spins out at the end of the phrase. The same device appears in the second verse, with *sin comprender*. (Also, note that this first verse, which begins by repeating the lie *que volverás*, that you will return, ends by accepting *que no volverás*, that you will not return. The verbal patterning in this stanza is quite compact.)

CHORUS

que me mientas—As in the verse, lying to oneself (or knowingly fantasizing) is the real theme here, the persistent setting or predicament of the song.

Then leave me me—This perhaps unusual phrase is my interpretation of the sentiment here; "Then leave me *be*" might suit some singers as an alternate translation preserving the vowels.

VERSE 2

ni qué mentir—The lies run out at the end of the song, along with the hopes and everything else but tears. This closure in the final words of the last phrase is perhaps the single interesting moment in an otherwise lackluster second verse; yet it also indicates the verse's overall weakness. With the song's main theme (self-deception) already exhausted, the only thing left is conventional stuff from central casting. *Ya ni sé qué hablar* (I'm running out of words) is all too true.

Malena (1942)

LYRICS: Homero Manzi
MUSIC: Lucio Demare

MALENA IS A towering image in the tango songbook—a mythical figure of the tango itself. She is also the evolution of the tango's earliest character, Milonguita. The hopeful flapper, who once worked the nightclubs looking for patronage and crying into her champagne, is here the singer who dominates the stage, bearing the entire city in her smokily voiced songs, animal and mineral, living and ghosts.

But who *is* Malena? Who was the real woman who now bares her soul eternally in the spotlight of this tango?

This question has had answers—or claimants, rather—since before it was even asked. One legend suggests Manzi wrote this song, like his other tango "Ninguna," as a tribute to Nelly Omar, the famous tango singer: she claimed as much herself. Many have pointed out, however, that the two only had an affair some time after "Malena" had already been written and recorded. Another story holds that Manzi heard a Chilean singer, under the stage name Malena de Toledo, during a trip to Brazil, and that he wrote the song for her; but this oft-repeated speculation seems quite at odds with the lyrics, preoccupied as they are with rootsy imagery of Buenos Aires and its outskirts. Other tales ask us to believe that Manzi raised this mythical figure in homage to an unknown chorus girl; or to an amalgam of women; or to his wife's dressmaker.

Any of these real life women could have been Malena; or none of them. Maybe the profusion of possibilities only proves how appealing the song is, and how eagerly we are seduced by its charismatic fiction. Perhaps Manzi wrote the lyrics to "Malena" as an imaginative portrait of the tango itself, its *canción* embodied in the striking figure of a woman who sings out her hurts through its words. The lyrics dig up many of the tango's early tropes—the *barro* or mud of the outskirts; the city girl shedding a tear over her champagne for the world she left behind; the various literary birds (larks and doves) that flit through her voice and hands—and the song also inverts the usual image of a woman in tango, by showing her looming above these details. Her song is now their source. She is art come to life, conquering circumstance.

Yet we are still left wondering where this portrait comes from. Thankfully, there is another possibile source for this mythical figure, which offers both a more credible origin, and one less wrapped up in personal vanity. And it has the added advantage of not reducing poetry to a gossip column.

The great Spanish poet and playwright Federico García Lorca was visiting Buenos Aires in the year 1933; and during his sojourn there, he delivered an influential lecture which would later become his famous essay *Juego y teoría del duende*—"Theory and Game of Duende." The ideas he explored, delving into the power of the uncanny and demonic, specifically related to the performing arts, exerted a deep influence on the arts throughout Latin America, then and now. Manzi's lyrics echo several of the essay's specific details, and on the whole, "Malena" is virtually a manifesto of Lorca's main theme: the hair-raising power of song. Manzi could have feasibly taken the name Malena from Lorca's essay as well, since a figure by that name appears there in connection with these potent images.

NOTES

VERSE 1

Malena—The name Malena, while common enough to have come from anywhere, was perhaps suggested to Manzi by a passage early in Lorca's essay "Teoría y juego del duende," where the Spanish poet mentions "the old Gypsy dancer La Malena" in a discussion of the black and gypsy elements in *duende*, or "possessed" performance.

ninguna—There is a somewhat tenuous possibility that Manzi's later tango "Ninguna," which he wrote for Nelly Omar, refers back to this line; but the reuse of this quite common word is more likely a mere coincidence.

A yuyo del suburbio su voz perfuma—While it is perfectly in keeping with tango imagery that Malena's voice would have the smell of "the grass of the outskirts," this also could be an echo of the closing sentence of Lorca's essay, where he relates the possessing *duende* to a wind blowing: *un aire con olor de saliva de niño, de hierba machacada* (a wind with the smell of a baby's spittle, of mashed grass).

aquel romance—This image of Malena reminiscing about a past romance while drinking is an echo of "Milonguita" while also a bit of a role reversal: usually in tangos it is the man who grows nostalgic while drinking. Cadícamo would soon paint a similar picture in "Los mareados."

voz de sombra—These particular words ("voice beshadowed" in my rendition) appear in Lorca's essay, as he describes the famous flamenco singer Pastora Pavón (1890-1969): *Jugaba con su voz de sombra, con su voz de estaño fundido, con su voz cubierta de musgo* (She toyed with her voice of shadow, with her voice of beaten tin, with her voice covered in moss).

CHORUS

la sal del recuerdo—The "salt of memory" is a clever metaphor, combining preservation (i.e., by salting) with tears.

te siento más buena… que yo—The speaker here is saying that Malena seems "better" (i.e., kinder, nobler) through her song than he is.

VERSE 2

sobre el barro del callejón—The mud of the alleys is an old element of tango iconography. It first enters the songbook with J. G. Castillo's opening lines in "Sobre el pucho" (1923):

> *Un callejón en Pompeya,*
> *y un farolito plateando el fango*
> (An alley down in Pompeya,
> And a streelight that shines the mud silver)

Manzi echoes this song more fully with his own "Barrio de tango," but its influence on his work is felt here in "Malena" too.

tus venas tienen sangre de bandoneón—Lorca asserts in his essay that *duende* is a matter not of skill but a thing *de sangre*, of the blood.

voz quebrada—This shattered or broken voice, a follow-up to the *voz de sombra* of the first verse, closely parallels the events related in the key anecdote of Lorca's essay. The flamenco singer Pastora Pavón at first toys with her *voz de sombra,* failing to interest her audience, before slamming a drink and breaking her voice to sing with *garganta abrasada* (scorched throat).

Pedacito de cielo (1942)

LYRICS: Homero Expósito
MUSIC: Enrique Francini & Héctor Stamponi

THE NEW LYRICISM of the 1940s found inspiration in "object poetry," as seeen in the tango "Tinta roja." This style's greatest talent was perhaps Homero Expósito, whose best work takes it to the pinnacle of the genre, this waltz being one such example.

In many ways, this kind of writing was just a further development of an earlier poetic: tango lyrics had used stock imagery, as well as stock characters and situations, from the beginning, some of it borrowed from the opera, some recycled from song to song. What happens in certain lyrics of the '40s is that the inanimate props come to dominate the storytelling, as the people recede, becoming vague background shadows, or else appear enormously enlarged as a single detail (such as the eye color in the second verse here). This poetic shift from people to details may well reflect a change in production: as songs were freed from their duty on stage and screen, and began to roam the airwaves detached from plays, perhaps their internal sense likewise became free from the narrative burden and could show a more liberated play of symbols.

VERSE 1

reja—The fence is said to be made of bronze in the second verse.

ojeras—Literally *ojeras* are dark circles under the eyes, an absolutely brilliant image for picturing the shadows at nightfall (under the windows, under the gate), albeit not the easiest to translate in as few words as the poetic line requires. Expóstio repeats this metaphor, as well as its off-rhyme with *hiedra* (ivy, vines), in the second verse. (In lunfardo, *ojeras* also means grudges or ill-will, perhaps a distant secondary meaning here.)

mi verso mejor—This mention of "my verse" suggests that the speaker in the song is the poet himself, or at least is a character in the same role. Curiously this is also the case in J. M. Contursi's waltz "Bajo un cielo de estrellas" of 1941, whose music was also composed by Francini and Stamponi, then working in the orchestra of Miguel Caló. This shift towards first-person lyrics in the mode of Petrarch is of course more marked in Contursi—as a poet, Expósito is always more elliptical than autobiographical—yet it seems to have been the general style of the '40s to adopt this angle, and to move away from the character-based concepts of previous decades.

CHORUS

Los años de la infancia—The focus here on childhood (*infancia*) may just be the story he wanted to tell; yet I detect in this detail the casual presence of a Freudian atmosphere, with its theory of childhood's indelible memories.

aquel beso robado al azar—Who "stole" the kiss from whom is left completely and beautifully ambiguous.

VERSE 2

Tal vez—The use of "perhaps" here, twice, and the indefinite imagery which follows in the last two phrases (where the grammar is somewhat ambiguous), places this entire verse in a more speculative mental arena, floating in a state of pure poetry; and perhaps because of that, less suited for singing.

azúcar quemada—Another brilliant metaphor for eyes, this "burnt sugar" color, with its sunset connotations, may also be a private reminiscence of *dulce de leche* or caramel, a particularly cherished sweet in Argentina.

Gricel (1942)

LYRICS: José María Contursi
MUSIC: Mariano Mores

THE TANGO "GRICEL" is the snapshot of a love affair which came to consume the inner life and career of José María Contursi, whose passion for the young Susana Gricel Viganó gave voice to many other tangos that share the imagery and longing of this one. Indeed Contursi's yearning for Gricel shapes his entire songbook, and is the overriding theme in lyrics written both before and after this one. Among the songs portraying the poet's passion we may count such well known tunes as "Cristal," "En esta tarde gris," "Toda mi vida," "Garras," "Más allá," "Y no puede ser," and "Tabaco." Perhaps without knowing it, Gricel had become the muse of the tango's most incandescent love poet, the distant Laura to his guilt-ridden Petrarch.

Contursi first met Gricel at a radio station, when the young girl was visiting her native Buenos Aires with some friends. She was then on a trip to the city from Córdoba, where her family had relocated for her father's health—and where Contursi was soon to travel on his own doctor's orders. The lyricist was then married, but pursued a brief love affair with the young girl, which was to dominate his mind for the rest of his life, leading to his many verses of longing and of broken hopes, and of the imagined call of his beloved, as she speaks to him like a ghost in his songs. The conventions of tango lyrics proved an effective mask for this poet's grief over lost love, and he bent its boundaries to make room for her voice, as in the refrain of this song.

Decades later, when Contursi was a widower and drinking himself through a deep depression, the two were fated to meet again. Gricel had also been left single, by her own husband's abandonment. The story goes that in 1962, bandoneonist Ciriaco Ortiz was traveling to his native Córdoba, and sought out Gricel to tell her the news about Contursi. She took a bus to Buenos Aires to meet her old flame right away, the first of many such trips. Within a few years, their reunion led to a second marriage for them both. Contursi enjoyed the last years of his life with her, after moving to Córdoba, and leaving the bottle behind.

Contursi himself considered "Gricel" the finest tango of his career, most surely from personal motives; and if others have long disagreed, that speaks less to this number in particular, than to the power and eloquence of his achievement as a songwriter.

VERSE 1

y sin embargo—The second and third phrase in each verse involve a change of melody, making them sound parenthetical, before the stanza resumes. Mores' melodic writing here quite aptly turns to advantage the uncommon five-phrase stanza of Contursi, who perhaps deserves more credit for his restless explorations of form within the bounds of normal song structure.

busqué... encontré... aturdí—Contursi repeats these rhymes (slightly varying their lines) in both verses, a device he used in several other lyrics as well. This use of a refrain, embedded within the verse, is specific to songs, and not much seen in other poetry; and while other tango lyricists used similar refrains and refrain-like patterning, Contursi made it something of a stylistic signature, using verbal repetition to underscore the obsessive thoughts and themes in his songbook.

Tu ilusión fue de cristal—Contursi was to reprise this metaphor two years later as the central image of his tango "Cristal."

CHORUS

No te olvides de mí—Contursi's use of dialogue here, letting Gricel speak in her own words, is uncommon in tangos. It seems to have been a favored device of his; he had already used a more extended instance of it, in his 1941 tango "En esta tarde gris," where the woman—the unnamed Gricel—speaks for an entire double-length chorus. There were tangos that used actual dialogue between two singers in the 1920s, but their banter is unlike Contursi's evocation (which is not dialogue but impersonation).

VERSE 2

Mi vida toda fue un engaño—The same feeling of self-deception (or living a lie) appears in other Contursi songs, notably "En esta tarde gris" (where the words *y mi engaño comprobé* are similarly tucked into the second verse). It is interesting to observe how Contursi's handling of the deceit motif, where it is internal to the speaker and reflects his own actions, differs from how others (Discépolo, Gorrindo, even Amadori) treated it during the 1930s, where the world is the big lie.

Mañana zarpa un barco (1942)

LYRICS: Homero Manzi
MUSIC: Lucio Demare

THIS HIT SONG from Lucio Demare and Homero Manzi (the duo behind "Malena") evokes the port scenery of Buenos Aires, *Dock Sud* in particular, where the Riachuelo flows along the riverbanks which, in former days, were lined with the city's slaughterhouses. The dock life of La Boca, the barrio at the mouth of the river, was also the subject of Argentina's premier Twentieth Century painter, Benito Quinquela Martín, mentioned earlier in connection with the tango "Caminito."

VERSE 1

la música del mar—Some sheet music printings read *música del mal* here, which would seem to be a misprint, except that certain singers actually performed it that way. The pronunciation might reflect a neighborhood accent, or could even represent a slip of the tongue. If the correction to *mar* is in fact wrong, the line might be translated:

> A hundred ports regale us with sounds of misery.

parece siempre igual—The opening four lines all rhyme, ending on the word *igual* ("the same"), to underline the monotony of the sailor's life.

CHORUS

Qué bien se baila—In the sheet music, the chorus is printed in halves (alternating 2 and 3 metrical beats), as shown here. Metrically the lines are similar to those of the chorus, but their rhythm is distinct, as in "Así se baila el tango."

VERSE 2

Al ritmo de su danza—Manzi's comparison between the rhythms of dance and sea is one of several moments in his songs where the tango dancing itself is part of the imagery. This occurs less often in tango lyrics than one might imagine. Manzi again evokes dancing directly in "Tal vez será mi alcohol" (1943) and "Discepolín" (1951).

Así se baila el tango (1942)

LYRICS: Marvil (Elizardo Martínez Vilas)
MUSIC: Elías Randal

THIS GIANT HIT from the orchestra of Ricardo Tanturi *y sus Indios* (and his Indians) put charismatic singer Alberto Castillo front and center—and sometimes down in the audience, as his bellicose delivery of the opening lines would sometimes start a quarrel with male listeners who took their mockery personally. (This apparently common occurrence was even dramatized in a film clip.) The cheeky lyrics by Marvil, known for his comic streak as a songwriter, illustrate the turf war of the times among different classes in society. While tango had been embraced by the upper classes since the early 1900s, its attitudes and its subject matter had always represented the dispossessed, the immigrant, the laborer. Songs like this one could be interpreted divisively, particularly when the tango was reaching its height of national popularity. The second verse, often missing from transcriptions, makes it pretty clear that song's main topic, of course, is the dance craze.

The Malena mentioned at the end of the refrain is the figure from the Homero Manzi tango. The lines may reflect a story, itself possibly fictional, that the real-life singer Malena de Toledo gave up her singing career when she learned that Manzi's tango had been written about her.

Of note in more recent times, this tango's title was used for the name of a televised instructional dance series, broadcast on Argentine television in the early 1990s, starring Osvaldo Zotto and Mora Godoy, which was a seminal part of the tango revival and brought tango dancing back into the national consciousness.

VERSE 1

Qué saben los pitucos—Lest the thrust of this famously provocative line be misunderstood, it expresses contempt not for high society but for conceit.

Así se corta el cesped—There may be some old slang joke in the phrase "to mow the lawn" (it possibly means to be snobbish); but it is more likely a simple play on words, stemming from the former use of *corte* (cut) to mean any fancy tango figure. The equivalent joke in English might be: "You just cut the grass, while I'm out cuttin' the rug." The alternate wording for this quip in some recordings simply substitutes the first words of the chorus: *Así se baila el tango, mientras dibujo* etc.

una corrida, una vuelta, una sentada—This actual sequence of moves, which quickly jumps from a frenetic run to a pose, is characteristic of the dancing seen in some 1940s films, although rather unlikely to be seen today.

CHORUS

Así se baila el tango—Despite the comic nature of these lyrics, this chorus presents what might be the least exaggerated picture of physical dancing one can find in a tango. The more pronounced delivery accentuates the beats in a slightly different way, drawing out the half-lines more, and thus asking for a different graphic treatment than the verse, although the two parts technically use the same meter.

Malena no cantó—Marvil's colorful story here, that the instruments of the band are sharing gossip about the characters in the songs, brings to life the way that themes and images were shared among tangos, as though the entire industry of song were a single gigantic soap opera.

VERSE 2

Será mujer o junco—This verse's joking turns from social scenery to one dancer's obsession, comically picturing various objects (a reed, machinery, a shadow or ghost) in place of a real partner. While the humor seems a little dated on paper, it probably applies pretty well to new dancers today, who are probably practicing with a grocery cart somewhere right now.

Los mareados (1942)

LYRICS: Enrique Cadícamo
MUSIC: Juan Carlos Cobián

THE DARINGLY ORIGINAL and widely beloved tango "Los mareados" is the result of a string of creative rewritings, spanning twenty years and involving several creative endeavors.

Originally composed as an instrumental tune called "Clarita" by Juan Carlos Cobián in the early 1920s, the song was given lyrics to become the title number of the show "Los Dopados" (The Stoners) by Raúl Doblas and Roberto Weisbach. The lyrics didn't stick as strongly as the new title, however, under which Osvaldo Fresedo recorded the song as an instrumental once again. In 1942, having become enamored of the melody, Aníbal Troilo brought the Fresedo disc over to the apartment of lyricist Enrique Cadícamo, insisting that he produce new lyrics so that the bandleader could add it to his repertoire. Despite Cadícamo's protest that Cobián was then on tour in the United States and would be unable to approve the rewriting, the revised song was debuted and recorded in 1942 under the new title "Los mareados." Literally the title means The Dizzy or The Woozy, but in context I prefer the more suggestive title here: The Wasted.

Cadícamo's immortal lyrics have nothing to do with the first text. The new song, with its depiction of drunken lovers bidding their failed fling a dizzy farewell, was censored by the military government in 1943 (like many other tangos of the era) for its portrayal of debauchery. The third stanza remained intact, thanks to which it was temporarily known by the title "En mi pasado."

As for the lyrics themselves, the opening stanza is justly famous, and is virtually made out of suggestive fumes. The opening words evoke an image of the woman sitting at a table, drinking, as the speaker luridly approaches, his description conveying his own intoxication. My translation makes some interpretive choices—as any must—and favors the song's vivid imagery over its strictly literal sense (which makes no sense at all).

VERSE

encendida—This suggestive word means "turned on," in multiple senses: on fire, inflamed, sexually aroused, lit up, and perhaps most commonly, switched on like a light. My translation strives to convey this ambiguous image contextually and cinematically, and to evoke the scene as a whole, more than any single, limited meaning. (After all, she is *como encendida*, "as if" turned on.)

el fragor del champán—This roar of champagne could refer to the crash of glasses or even to corks popping. More generally, it suggests the roar of troubled emotion or noisy environment. In any case, it gives the song a particularly hallucinatory quality.

por no llorar—The conjunction of champagne and tearshed here is an echo of "Milonguita," especially considering the scene of parting lovers. Many of Cadícamo's lyrics (e.g., "En la buena y en la mala") are steeped in this casino-and-nightclub atmosphere of the early tangos. (It was common to the period, and a prominent setting in John Galsworthy's widely read novels of *The Forsyte Saga*, serialized 1906-1921.)

tus bellos ojos—Variants of this line include *lindos ojos* (as Fiorentino sang) and *negros ojos* (as Goyeneche sang).

CHORUS

Esta noche, amiga mia—This may be too fine a point; but I notice the elisions in these first four lines of the chorus lend themselves to being slurred, or delivered in a tipsy manner. My translation has a bit of this too, albeit far less than Cadícamo's wording (as I understand it).

los mareados—As noted above, *mareado* means dizzy or woozy. In the context of the song, however, I choose *wasted*, in part for narrative reasons: no one in a bar would laugh at calling people *dizzy*.

tenemos—This triple rhyme (*tenemos - beberemos - volveremos*) suggests a particularly drunken quality, and underlines the state of the speaker as a participant in the action he describes.

TRIO

en mi pasado—This stanza gave the song its alternate title "En mi pasado," during the censorship years beginning in 1943, due to the absence of any references to alcohol in these lines.

nuevas sendas tomaremos—Compared to other "breakup songs" in the genre, this ending is relatively kind in sentiment. There is a gentle wink of irony in the verb used here too, with the former lovers to "take" (*tomar*) their separate ways just as they were taking shots of liquor before.

Percal (1943)

LYRICS: Homero Expósito
MUSIC: Domingo Federico

PERHAPS THE CLEAREST example of tangos "talking to each other" across the years occurs in the impressionistic lyrics of "Percal." The song is a retelling of the famous 1920 tango "Milonguita," from the perspective of a man left behind in the outskirts of the metropolis; and he seems to be a different character from the one who sings the earlier tango. His remove from the events he describes is part of the story, and Expósito carefully echoes the wording of the old song in his own.

As is the case in many of his other lyrics, Expósito here builds his song around a handful of objects—her old dress, a path, a house—along with remembered emotions and phrases that suggest conflict or even scandal, such as *Tal vez nos enteramos mal* (Perhaps we heard the story wrong). This type of "poetry on the periphery" bears a certain resemblance to the introspective, associative lyricism which appears in the literary poetry of the time, and which many readers nowadays link to Proust.

VERSE 1

Percal...—The fine weave of cotton fabric once used for women's house dresses. The word's associations with a simple domestic life, contrasted to the silken life of luxury, are most famously registered in the chorus of "Milonguita." (See note on the word *percal* there for more details.)

Te acuerdas—This wording quotes the opening line of "Milonguita" (*Te acordás, Milonguita?*) in a manner that will seem coincidental to no one familiar with both songs.

quince abriles—The girl's fifteen years of age (fifteen Aprils) may be an echo of Massenet's *Manon*, whose protagonist is fifteen when she enters a life of luxury and debauchery. The detail is not included in "Milonguita."

nos enteramos mal—This mention of people hearing about the girl's life in rumors creates a social background in a single swift stroke. It functions similarly to Cadícamo's evoking "what other people say" in his lyrics (see "Los mareados" and "Rondando tu esquina").

CHORUS

tirados—These multiple rhymes in quick succession, like those at the end of the chorus, occur at a moment of heightened dramatic tension, and seem to have been a favorite device of Expósito. They also appear prominently in the lyrics of Cátulo Castillo ("Tinta roja" in this volume, and especially "La ultima curda" of 1956). Such cascades of rhyme perhaps came into vogue among songwriters during the peak years of the Golden Age.

VERSE 2

Llorar—This stanza picks up where "Milonguita" leaves off ("When you cry, they all blame the champagne.")

Saber—In parallel with the opening of this verse, the infinitive here suggests that the girl is the one whose fate it is "to know" that she suffers, that she will never forget her past, etc.—yet grammatically the wording extends this to the speaker and the audience too.

Esta noche de luna (1943)

LYRICS: Héctor Marcó

MUSIC: Graciano Gómez & José García

NOTES

LYRICIST HÉCTOR MARCÓ was a frequent songwriting collaborator of the masterful Carlos Di Sarli, with whom he coauthored a number of tunes. The typical Marcó lyric suited the orchestra handsomely: his songs have little social commentary, and seldom delve into the darker corners of the soul, but they carry a tune perfectly and they establish not just a romantic atmosphere but deliver the experience of romance. If Marcó does not quite measure up to the more substantial poetic gifts of Manzi, Expósito, Contursi, or Discépolo (and in fairness, few do), and if he never quite wrote of the neighborhoods and other nostalgic tango themes, he yet remains the unrivaled master of the soaring, operatic tango—not the center but rather the aspiration of the genre.

This 1943 hit delivers all of that and more. With themes modeled on the famous barcarolle from Offenbach's opera *Les Contes d'Hoffmann* (1881), Marcó turns the basic premise—*Belle nuit, ô nuit d'amour* (Beautiful night, O night of love)—into a single lover's serenade, steering the tango idiom into a three-minute *opéra fantastique*.

VERSE 1

Acércate a mi—This verse form is unusual for a tango, and each pair of short lines could also be set as a single long one.

un brujo reloj—The "sorcerer's clock" of this metaphor is perhaps an allusion to the automaton Olympia in *Les Contes d'Hoffmann* (or may recall the Talking Turk from Hoffmann's short story "The Automaton"). In any case, it gives the entire song an aura of the fantastic, suggesting the speaker is not real without completely committing to that premise.

nos redimirá—The idea that the lovers should be "redeemed" or liberated begs the question: redeemed from what? Again, it suggests that the speaker is not real, or at least pictures himself craving the fulfillment of real life, like another Pinocchio. The alternate wording for this line in some editions (*nos revivirá,* shall revive us) only underscores this matter.

BRIDGE 1

barcarola—The barcarola or barcarolle is the song of Venetian gondoliers, and its later imitation, which became a fashionable type of romantic song throughout the 1800s. The most famous one is from Offenbach's opera *Les Contes d'Hoffmann* (1881), "Belle nuit, ô nuit d'amour"—which Marcó's lyrics are very deliberately recalling.

CHORUS

Soy una estrella en el mar—Like the earlier suggestion that the speaker is a robot or Pinocchio figure who is not entirely real (see above), this star metaphor dips into a type of fantasy not often seen in tangos.

VERSE 2

El canto del mar—Based on what this song of the sea actually says ("what a night full of love"), it seems pretty clear that the song Marcó has in mind is Offenbach's barcarolle.

Nada (1944)

LYRICS: Horacio Sanguinetti
MUSIC: José Dames

STORIES UNFOLD ELLIPTICALLY in many tangos, and this one uses just a few glimpses of detail to tell of a man's journey out to the country, in search of a former beloved whose empty house has been overtaken by cobwebs. With nothing to greet him but the padlock on the door, he prays before its temporary crucifix.

"Nada" is hardly the only tango whose harrowing lyrics are set in a major key (B-flat in this case); but it is certainly one of the most effective at creating tension out of the contrast between the tune and the text. The melody in the verse is hopeful and perhaps even jaunty, conveying the traveler's optimism. The chorus, rather than disputing this by shifting to a minor key, continues it almost ironically, as the protagonist faces the abandoned house that stands before him instead of his expected old-time flame.

VERSE 1

Si me han dicho—As in Cadícamo's lyrics, this mention of the speech of others quickly sketches in a social background for the song.

Cuánta nieve hay en mi alma—This image of snow perhaps correlates to the setting, which is presumably in the Argentine interior near the Andes.

un candado de dolor—This padlock of sorrow is the central image of the song, communicating bereavement to both the speaker and the listener. Unlike the locked doors in mystery and adventure tales, which often suggest temptation, this one conceals exactly what the title announces—emptiness.

CHORUS

El rosal—These lines in the chorus might be organized in a number of other ways, but I follow the delivery of most singers and break them into shorter segments.

hoy he vuelto arrepentido—The speaker/lover's claim that he has repented, implying the innocence of the beloved, is the distinguishing theme of the 1940s tangos compared to the genre's earlier phases.

VERSE 2

la cruz de tu candado—Sanguinetti's further development of this symbol seems to have entirely poetic motives, but may have been suggested by the mechanical form of a "cruciform lock" (i.e., a lock whose keyhole is shaped like a cross).

Llueve otra vez (1944)

LYRICS: Oscar Rubens

MUSIC: Juan José Guichandut

THE CINEMATIC LYRICS of "Llueve otra vez" return to a setting shared by many tangos that brood on romantic separation: the rain and fog of the port city. Indeed, perhaps because the precedent of these foul-weather backgrounds was so well established, its authors telegraphed their borrowing of the subject by making the title of this song "Rain falls *once again*"—words which, in a rare event for a tango, do not actually occur in the lyrics.

Strangely, in another tale of absences, the name of lyricist Oscar Rubens is omitted from the 1944 sheet music score of "Llueve otra vez," and is also absent from both shellac discs pressed during the Golden Age in that same year—the recordings made by the orchestras of Pedro Laurenz (with Carlos Bermudez singing) and of Carlos Di Sarli (with Alberto Podestá singing). Further examples of odd documentation: Rubens' name is also missing from discs of the songs "Canta, pajarito" and "Tarareando," which he also cowrote with Guichandut (who is credited with the lyrics). Rubens and Guichandut are both named on the 1944 Odeon disc of "Domingo a la noche," featuring the orchestra of Miguel Caló with Raúl Berón on vocals; but this time Guichandut's middle initial is wrong. All these errors notwithstanding, Rubens is duly registered with SADAIC as the lyricist of these songs, and his name is credited properly in later publications.

VERSE 1

Escucha—As in "Percal" and "Garras," the opening phrase in the verse here mixes sustained notes and rests, to elongate a few words through the measures of this phrase. Musical notation being absent in this volume, I denote the extra time value with ellipses (which are not printed in the 1944 edition of the sheet music I consulted). This extended rhythmic device, which one might call a verbal *pesante* mode, occurs in the first and third phrases of both verses. Rubens uses the exact same form in "Calla bandoneón," also published in 1944; and the sheet music for that song does include ellipses.

CHORUS

Llueve—Curiously, the words *llueve otra vez* do not actually occur in the lyrics, although rain is mentioned obsessively. For these words to be used as the song's title, without being extracted from the vocal line, is a relatively rare occurrence in tango. As in jazz and indeed most forms of popular song, a song's most memorable words would usually be preferred for titling, simply as good practice in a competitive market; and songs were often renamed by audiences where they did not adhere to this convention initially.

relámpago de fiebre loca—This line appears in parentheses in the 1944 sheet music, which I choose not to follow. It is pretty obvious that this line is restating the previous one; and I suspect that the parentheses were added to clarify the delivery, for the kind of impromptu performances which were more common during the golden age of radio broadcasting.

VERSE 2

Mañana—The reassuring sentiment expressed at the end of this song is rather uncommon in tangos as a genre; and if the chorus were repeated after this second verse, its uplifting message would also be washed away in a veritable downpour of unhappy longing. Cases like this offer a good example of how repeats can play a very dynamic role in song, in ways not usually available to printed poetry. Here the song's own stanzas, like opposite faces of a coin, allow and indeed require the performer to choose what sense they will ultimately convey.

Garras (1944)

LYRICS: José María Contursi
MUSIC: Aníbal Troilo

CONTURSI'S LYRICS FOR "Garras," a portrait of the harrowed and haunted lover, has two notable features, besides a certain memorable punchiness. First, in the verse, the phrases evoke coldness by the use of abundant rests—except in the third phrase, which rattles out a more verbose complaint, before subsiding into the coldness and quiet from which it emerged. Secondly, the chorus makes a sudden shift of background scenery from darkened urban alleys, which are nothing new in a tango, to the world of folktales and superstition, by evoking the goblin-like *duende* as a metaphor for the speaker, and introducing the song's titular image of rending claws.

VERSE 1

Ansias de vivir—This second phrase, also in the second verse, is printed as a single line in the edition of the sheet music approved for radio broadcast (EDAMI, 1945). This misrepresents its rhythmic value; however, such a layout is obviously a concession to the space available at the bottom of the page. My arrangement, by comparison, gives equal space to equal tempo. (See also the note below on *Y me ha quedado*.)

CHORUS

era un duende errabundo—The *duende* (goblin or, colloquially in my translation, fiend) is a house-spirit in Andalusian folklore, derived from the ancient tradition of household gods or *lares* (to use the Roman name) present in many early cultures. In more modern times, such dieties, similarly to fairies and sprites, have been represenations of mischief; Contursi's image is more likely meant to suggest a feeling of homelessness, since the spirit is *errabundo* (wandering). The word *duende* also relates to the sense of irrational, daemonic possession which descends upon performers and which captivates audiences, as detailed in García Lorca's influential essay "Juego y teoría del duende," which he first delivered as a lecture in Buenos Aires in 1933. (For more on this essay and its influence on the tango, see also my notes on "Malena.")

Y me ha quedado—In the 1945 edition of the sheet music, the phrase breaks here in order to highlight the *quedado - abandonado* rhyme, rather than to respect the rhythmic structure of the lines (as favored in my arrangements).

que se agarran como garras y desgarran—This type of replete wordplay is uncommon in tangos, and is perhaps even in poor taste; except that the verbal repetition, by its very crudeness, helps to evoke a certain psychological experience of brutality.

Este llanto tuyo—These words obviously mean "this crying (of mine) over you," as opposed to "this crying you perform." See my note on the chorus of "Rondando tu esquina" for a similar reading of *tu amor* in that lyric.

Rondando tu esquina (1945)

LYRICS: Enrique Cadícamo

MUSIC: Charlo (Carlos José Pérez de la Riestra)

DESCRIBED BY SOME as the ultimate distillation of romantic desire, "Rondando tu esquina" was destined to shed its tango stylings to become an immense hit throughout Latin America, often as a bolero. The song boasts fresh recordings in every decade from the 1940s up to the present. In Mexico alone, it has been recorded no fewer than 60 times.

On a side note, these non-tango renditions demonstrate how songs on sad themes are perhaps not the simple effusions of melancholy which they are sometimes thought to be; because these other recordings are positively cheerful. The tango is content to brood, or to seem to; but under the surface there is an aspect of these songs which is subtly competitive. It is as though by flaunting how intensely one suffers for the beloved, the song performs a kind of mating dance.

The lyrics come from the hand of Enrique Cadícamo, who by then had twenty years of hit songs to his credit; and the music was composed by the great tango singer Charlo, who wrote a handful of other sophisticated and original melodies, including "Fueye," "Ave de paso," "Tu pálida voz" and "El viejo vals." The present song was immediately recorded by two of the tango's most talented orchestras—that of Ángel D'Agostino, with vocals by Ángel Vargas; and that of Osvaldo Pugliese, with vocals by Roberto Chanel (whose rendition alters a few words, as detailed below).

VERSE 1

Esta noche—In the Pugliese-Chanel rendition this line is altered to:

Esta noche tengo ganas de olvidarla,
sin embargo que ansias loca de buscarla

The altered wording is largely borrowed from the second verse, which is not sung in their recording.

Ya no me importa el que diran—As in other Cadícamo lyrics, this quick stroke ("what other people say") establishes a fictive social world behind the speaker. He uses a similar device in the chorus of "Nostalgias."

CHORUS

vida mia—A term of endearment for a lover; yet in this instance, it is also a rhetorical gesture the speaker makes towards his fate.

tu amor—"Your love" is, of course, the love the speaker feels towards his beloved. (See also note to "Garras," *Este llanto tuyo*.)

VERSE 2

La mariposa del dolor—I have not been able to determine whether this "butterfly of pain" (or moth of grief) has a simple meaning in slang (*mariposa* meaning a lady of the night, or a flirt generally), or if it refers to something outside the song (such as some event in a play potentially surrounding this tune); but it makes for a rather animated metaphor in any case.

noche de verbena—A *verbena* is a street celebration with open-air dancing, usually held on the eve of a saint's day.

Tu íntimo secreto (1945)

LYRICS: Héctor Marcó
MUSIC: Graciano Gómez

THE MARCÓ-GÓMEZ SONGWRITING duo reconvened to write this follow-up hit to their 1943 smash "Esta noche de luna." Like their earlier outing, this song's tone is sentimental and largely positive, and gives the singer a fine platform to indulge in more swooning, romantic repertoire. Marcó also turns here to imagery reminiscent of fairy tales and lyrical opera, a strain in which he seems to have been quite at home.

As is also the case with other tangos written in long lines (such as "Mano a mano"), the lines of the verse here could well be arranged in halves instead. The melody, however, runs these segments together into longer, unbroken statements. The same thing occurs in the verse of Marcó's earlier "Esta noche de luna"; and as in that song, the chorus here opens with a long note held on a monosyllable: *Ven...* (Come...) The effect of this sustained vowel is amplified by the more verbose flowing lines that come before and after.

VERSE 1

La dicha es un castillo—Besides establishing a background of fairy-tale imagery for this song, this line functions like a refrain at the beginning and end of each verse. This structural device was one Marcó favored in the 1940s, and he also uses it in "Esta noche de luna" and "Nido gaucho," among others.

Acércame tus labios—This wording conspicuously echoes "Esta noche de luna," the big hit Marcó and Gómez had written the previous year.

CHORUS

Ven, mira que hermosa está la luna—Another echo of "Esta noche de luna."

VERSE 2

un globo de papel—Paper lanterns (or hanging lampshades) feature in several other tangos, and were a common feature of cabaret decor.

INDEX OF FIRST LINES

This index lists the first line of every stanza (verse, chorus, etc.), since some readers may know or wish to find certain tunes by particular sections.

Acaricia mi ensueño . . . 42
Acércate a mi: y oirás mi corazón. . . . 90, 92
Alley in the dark, night that never ends . . . 99
Alley in the dark, waiting still for you . . . 99
Alma, que en pena vas errando . . . 26
And tomorrow, when you hit the curb like last year's decorations . . . 23
Así aprendí (que hay qué fingir) . . . 32
Así se baila el tango . . . 80
As you step in the dark of the morning . . . 19
Aún el tiempo no logró . . . 26
Boundary wall (your red ink in the gray of the past) . . . 59, 61
By your moan, bandoneón . . . 47
Callejón sin luz, esperándote . . . 98
Callejón sin luz, noche sin final . . . 98
Caminito que el tiempo ha borrado . . . 24
Caminito que todas las tardes . . . 24
Come, and see how pretty the moon is . . . 103
Come closer to me, and hear my heart dance . . . 91, 93
Corre, corre, barcarola . . . 90, 92
Cry, bandoneón, your tango gray. . . . 53
Cuando sales por la madrugada . . . 18
Déjame mentir que volverás. . . . 62
Desde que se fue. . . . 24
Dónde estará mi arrabal . . . 58
Don't you stop thinking of me . . . 75
Dos meses en un barco viajó mi corazón . . . 78

INDEX

Do you recall, Milonguita? You once were 19
El día que me quieras. 42, 44
En la luz de unos ojos divinos 38
Esa voz que vuelvo a oír 28
Escucha corazón. 96
Esta noche, amiga mía 84
Esta noche tengo ganas de buscarla. 100
Este pobre corazón que no la olvida 100
Estercita (hoy te llaman Milonguita) 18
Esthercita (now they call you Milonguita) 19
Even time was of no use 27
Fevered, shaky Twentieth Century (hockshop fit to collapse) 37
For two months on the ocean, my heart shipped out alone 79
Fue tu voz, bandoneón 46
Gime, bandoneón, tu tango gris 52
Going crackers in my sadness, I get thinking back on you 21
He llegado hasta tu casa. 94
Here's to you, my old companion. 85
Here tonight I have an urge to go and find her 101
Honeysuckle in bloom, you saw when I was born. 31, 33
How nice a feeling, to dance on terra firma 77
Hoy resulta que es lo mismo (ser derecho que traidor) 34
Hoy tenés el mate lleno de infelices ilusiones. 20
Hoy vas a entrar en mi pasado 84
Hurry, hurry, barcarola 91, 93
I am a star on the sea 91
I'd had enough, and in my rush to be done 99
Igual que vos soñé 48
In the light of those eyes shining holy. 39
I once made fun of you 47
It's toying with my daydreams 43
I've come to learn (you must pretend) 33
I've got to see you one more time. 55
I've not a scrap to thank you for, fair and square we ended 21
I want to get my heart completely drunk 51
La casa tenía una reja. 70
La dicha es un castillo con un puente de cristal. 102
La juventud se fue 86
La noche que me quieras 44

Leave me here to lie that you'll return. 63
Life of mine, what have you brought me. 101
Like you I had a dream 49
Listen how, my heart 97
Little pathway that once in the evenings. 25
Little pathway that time now has faded 25
Llorar (por qué vas a llorar) 88
Llueve (y un látigo de luz me azota) 96
Long I waited for you unaware. 65
Los años de la infancia pasaron, pasaron 70
Madreselvas en flor, que me vieron nacer 30, 32
Malena canta el tango como ninguna 66
Malena sings the tango like no one else does. 67
Meanwhile, may your winnings, your poor momentary winnings. . . . 23
Me faltó después tu voz 74
Mientras tanto, que tus triunfos, pobres triunfos pasajeros. 22
Muchachos (si cualquiera de estas noches) 38, 40
Mucho te esperé sin comprender. 64
My buddies (if on any of these evenings) 39, 41
Nada debo agradecerte, mano a mano hemos quedado 20
Nada, nada queda en tu casa natal 94
Never should I once have thought 75
Night by night my memories of you 57
Noche que consigues envolver 56
No debi pensar jamás. 74
No pude más, y en mi afán por llegar 98
Nostalgias (de escuchar su risa loca) 50
Nostalgias (for how her crazy laughter sounded) 51
Not a thing is left in your childhood home 95
No te olvides de mi. 74
Now you must enter my past life 85
Now youth has gone away. 87
Off I go from where your house was 95
Old boundary wall (around the slums) 31
Out I came to where your house is 95
Paredón (tinta roja en el gris del ayer) 58, 60
Pasaron los años 32
Percal (te acuerdas del percal) 86
Percale (do you remember the percale) 87

INDEX

Qué bien se baila sobre la tierra firme . . . 76
Que el mundo fue y será (una porquería ya lo sé) . . . 34
Qué falta de respeto (qué atropello a la razón) . . . 36
Que me has dado, vida mia . . . 100
Qué saben los pitucos, lamidos y shushetas . . . 80
Qué te importa que te llore . . . 62
Quiero emborrachar mi corazón . . . 50
Quiero verte una vez más . . . 54
Rain falls (and the whips of light go lashing) . . . 97
Rara, como encendida . . . 84
Rechiflado en mi tristeza, te evoco y veo que has sido . . . 20
Riberas que no cambian tocamos al anclar . . . 76
Se dio el juego de remanye cuando vos, pobre percanta . . . 20
Será mujer o junco, cuando hace una quebrada . . . 82
Siglo veinte, cambalache (problemático y febril) . . . 36
Since she went away . . . 25
Soon I came to miss your voice . . . 75
Soul, as in sorrow you go straying . . . 27
Soy (una estrella en el mar) . . . 90
Tal vez se enfrió con la brisa . . . 72
Tarde que me invita a conversar . . . 54
Te acordás, Milonguita? Vos eras . . . 18
That same voice I hear again . . . 29
That's how you dance the tango . . . 81
That the world has been and will always be (a pigsty, that I knew) . . . 35
The breeze perhaps chilled ever after . . . 73
The day you ever love me . . . 43, 45
The guessing game was up when you were just a poor young doll . . . 21
The house had an old metal fencing . . . 71
The night you ever love me . . . 45
The ritzy, what do they know, the pretty boys and hipsters . . . 81
The season of our childhood has passed on . . . 71
The sorrows that left behind . . . 97
This poor heart of mine that can't forget about her . . . 101
Through your song (runs the chill of a final encounter) . . . 67
To cry (what makes you want to cry) . . . 89
Today it all turns out the same (to be faithful or a façade) . . . 35
Today your bonnet's all abuzz with madcap expectations . . . 21
Tristeza que dejó . . . 96

True bliss is like a castle with a bridge made out of glass 103
Tu canción (tiene el frío del ultimo encuentro) 66
Tus ojos son oscuros como el olvido 68
Twilights always summon me to speak 55
Ven, mira que hermosa está la luna 102
Vieja pared (del arrabal) 30
Weirdly, as in a spotlight 85
We touch down when we anchor on banks that never change 77
What disrespect for decency (what a trampling on the books) 37
What's your worry that I'm crying 63
Where did my old hood go 59
Will it be a reed or woman, when breaking into poses 83
Ya me alejo de tu casa. 94
Years have gone by now 33
Y mañana, cuando seas descolado mueble viejo 22
Yo me burlé de vos 46
Your eyes are in a darkness of things forgotten 69

INDEX OF TITLES

Alma del bandoneón. 46
Alma en pena 26
A Ship Sails Out Tomorrow 77
Así se baila el tango 80
Cambalache 34
Caminito 24
Claws 99
Don't Go Asking Me Why 39
El día que me quieras 42
Esta noche de luna 90
Fair and Square 21
Garras 98
Gricel. 74
Gricel 75
Hanging Round Your Corner 101
Hockshop 35
Honeysuckle 31
I've Got to See You One More Time 55
Little Pathway. 25
Llueve otra vez. 96
Los mareados 84
Madreselva 30
Malena 66
Malena 67
Mano a mano 20
Mañana zarpa un barco 76
Milonguita 18
Milonguita. 19
Nada 94

No me pregunten por qué 38
Nostalgias 50
Nostalgias 51
Nothing. 95
Pedacito de cielo 70
Percal. 86
Percale 87
Qué te importa que te llore. 62
Quiero verte una vez más 54
Rain Falls Once Again 97
Red Ink 59
Rondando tu esquina 100
Small Piece of Heaven 71
Soul in Sorrow 27
Soul of the Bandoneón. 47
That's How You Dance the Tango 81
The Day You Ever Love Me 43
The Wasted 85
This Night Full of Moonlight 91
Tinta roja 58
Tu íntimo secreto 102
What's Your Worry that I'm Crying 63
Your Innermost of Secrets 103

JAKE SPATZ is a poet, freelance editor, and independent scholar, whose work as a literary translator focuses on Italian poetry and Argentine tango. His verse translations of tango lyrics have been featured regularly since 2020 on the radio program *Bienvenidos al tango*, broadcast weekly on WOWD-LP, Takoma Park. He has also presented his research on tango lyrics and their cultural background in a series of lectures, sponsored by the Philadelphia Argentine Tango School. He is translator of the *Cantos* of Giacomo Leopardi (2022) and editor of the *Complete Poems* of James Thomson (B. V.) (2012). His translations also include selections from Dante and modern Italian poets, and his singable translations include selections from operas by Mozart, Rossini, and Puccini. He studied literature, philosophy, and filmmaking at Sarah Lawrence College (BA, 1999), and founded TangoDC in 2005. He currently teaches and runs tango events in Washington, DC.

BEATRIZ DUJOVNE was born and raised in Buenos Aires, and has lived much of her adult life in the Midwest and Pacific Northwest of the United States. A member of the American Psychological Association, she received a degree in Clinical Psychology from the University of Buenos Aires, and a Ph.D. in Counseling Psychology from the University of Missouri. Her book *In Strangers' Arms: The magic of the tango* (2011) is the first work in English to be endorsed by the National Tango Academy of Buenos Aires. She is also the author of *"Don't Be Sad When I'm Gone": A memoir of loss and healing in Buenos Aires* (2020), and dances avidly in Argentina and her home in Portland, OR.

PUBLISHED BY
CHARLES & WONDER
CHSWDR.COM

www.ingramcontent.com/pod-product-compliance
Lightning Source LLC
Chambersburg PA
CBHW030531310726
48979CB00010B/1881/J